"A GUIDE TO CULTIVATING A HEALTHY, NURTURING AND ENDURING MARITAL RELATIONSHIP

By

TRACY PHILIPS

Published by ITGM Publishing Inc., St. Louis, MO 63136

In Greek, several words encompass different types and nuances of love they are

Agape Love

in the New Testament, the fatherly love of God for humans, as well as the human reciprocal love for God. In Scripture, the transcendent agape love is the highest form of love and is contrasted with eros, or erotic love, and philia, or brotherly love.

Eros Love

Eros is physical love or sexual desire. Eros is the type of love that involves passion, lust, and/or romance. Examples of eros would be the love felt between, well, lovers. Eros is the sensual love between people who are sexually attracted to each other.

Philia Love

Philia love is the love of friendship. In Greek, philia means brotherly love. It originated from Aristotle's ethics but has been used in different contexts since Storage LoveThe Enhanced Strong's Lexicon defines storage love as "cherishing one's kindred, especially parents or children; the mutual love of parents and children and wives and husbands; loving affection;

prone to love; loving tenderly; chiefly of the reciprocal tenderness of parents and children.

Pragma Love

Pragma is a love that is seen in many long-term marriages and friendships. It is built on commitment, endurance, companionship, and sharing similar hopes for the future, which includes things like building a family and putting down roots.

Table of Contents

DEDICATION

To the enduring power of love, the strength of commitment, and the beauty of partnership. To every couple who has faced challenges, navigated storms, and emerged stronger on the other side. Tracy made this book as a guide to deepen your connection and strengthen your bond. To the enduring call of love the strength of commitment and the Beauty of partnership. This book is dedicated to all those who believe in the transformative potential of a healthy, nurturing, and enduring marital relationship.

It is for the dreamers who aspire to build a life filled with love, respect, and unwavering support. To my beloved significant other, whose unwavering love and unwavering belief in the institution of marriage, have been my constant source of inspiration. This book is a testament to the depth of our connection, and the journey we have undertaken together.

To the individuals who dream of finding their soulmate and embarking on a lifelong journey of love. This book is a roadmap to help you build a foundation that will withstand the test of time. To the families and communities that support and uplift the institution of marriage, may this book offer valuable insight into fostering healthy relationships and nurturing the love that binds us all together. And finally, to the countless stories of enduring love, and the infinite possibilities of a loving partnership. This book is dedicated with the hope that it may contribute in some small way to a world filled with loving and enduring marriages.

With love and dedication, Tracy C Phillips,

ENDORSEMENTS

I am thrilled and wholeheartedly endorse "A Guide to A Healthy, Nurturing, And Enduring Marital Relationship " written by Tracy C. Phillips. This book is a remarkable and invaluable resource for anyone, seeking to build a strong and lasting bond with their partner. In today's fast-paced world maintaining a happy and fulfilled marriage can be a challenging endeavor. However, Tracy Phillips has provided readers with a comprehensive and practical guide that offers guidance, wisdom, and insight into the complexities of modern relationships.

What sets this book apart is its commitment to addressing not only the superficial aspects of marital happiness but also delving deep into the emotional, psychological, and spiritual dimensions of a partnership. Tracy Phillips understands that a successful marriage is not just about resolving conflicts or maintaining appearances but about fostering genuine connection and intimacy.

Throughout the book, readers will find a treasure trove of advice on communication, conflict resolution trust building, and the importance of self-care within a marriage. The author skillfully navigates the delicate balance between individuality, and togetherness, emphasizing that a strong partnership is built on the strength of two whole individuals. In conclusion "A Guide to a Healthy Nurturing and Enduring Marital Relationship" is a must-read for anyone who values their partnership and seeks to cultivate a deep lasting connection with their spouse. Tracy Phillips's expertise, empathy, and genuine desire to help couples thrive shine through in every chapter. I wholeheartedly, endorse this book as an essential resource for building and maintaining a loving and enduring marital relationship. It is a true gem that will, undoubtedly enrich the lives of those who read it.

By Jeremy Phillips

"A Guide to a Healthy, Nurturing, and Enduring Marital Relationship" by Tracy C. Phillips generates thought-provoking insights for couples young and old who are seeking a better romantic or marital relationship. A path to self-reflection along with learning how to consider your mate's feelings and thoughts. Also building trust with honest communication and empathy is stressed throughout the book which can help lead couples to become less judgmental and confrontational.

By Lester L. Branch

In reading this book by Miss Tracy Phillip the author brings about an enrichment of the person who will take the amount of their time to receive the gifted work of learning about what love is. And how it transforms those who ingest its' virtue into their person, they become marvelous human beings. This is a superb book for learning about true love, which is in the Greek language spelled in five different ways with five different meanings, by Miss Phillip. The author will explain it in her book and it will be very clear and certain for the reader to understand, which is very profound in her written discourse.

INTERNATIONAL TRUE GOSPEL MINISTRIES, INC. I.T. G.M. Publishing Company
Professor LeMoyne Brown Sr., Ph.D., Th.D., D.D.

INTRODUCTION

Cultivating a healthy, nurturing, and enduring marital relationship is a journey that requires dedication, communication, and mutual respect. At its core, a successful marriage is built upon a foundation of open and honest communication. Partners should feel comfortable discussing their thoughts, feelings, and concerns, fostering an environment where misunderstandings can be resolved before they escalate. Effective communication also entails active listening, which involves giving undivided attention to one another and demonstrating empathy. Through sharing both joys and challenges, couples can create a deep sense of emotional intimacy that strengthens their bond. Nurturing a marital relationship involves the intentional practice of kindness and appreciation.

Small gestures of affection, like leaving notes of encouragement or spending quality time together, can go a long way in fostering closeness. Partners need to prioritize each other's well-being and personal growth. This involves supporting individual interests and aspirations, and recognizing that a strong marriage thrives when both individuals continue to evolve and fulfill their potential. By nurturing shared experiences and creating new memories, couples can keep the spark alive and reinforce the reasons they came together in the first place.

Endurance in a marital relationship is a testament to the commitment and resilience of both partners. Challenges are inevitable, but couples who view difficulties as opportunities for growth can emerge even stronger. The ability to compromise and find common ground is vital, as is the practice of forgiveness. Letting go of past mistakes and focusing on the present and future can prevent resentment from festering. Patience and a long-term perspective are key, as marriages, like any lasting endeavor, require time to weather storms and enjoy the sunshine. Through continuous effort, a healthy and nurturing marital relationship can stand the test of time, providing a source of comfort, companionship, and love for years to come.

CHAPTER 1: THE FOUNDATION OF LOVE

The foundation of love is a profound and intricate blend of emotions, actions, and connections that form the cornerstone of human relationships. At its core, love emerges from a deep sense of empathy, understanding, and acceptance for another individual, it begins with the recognition of shared values interests, and experiences, fostering a sense of camaraderie and emotional resonance As people engage in meaningful conversations and spend time together, they unveil their vulnerabilities, allowing for genuine connections to be established. These connections pave the way for trust to develop, serving as a vital pillar of love's foundation Trust is built through consistent and reliable actions that demonstrate one's commitment and sincerity creating a safe space where both partners can be their authentic selves without fear of Judgment. Alongside trust effective communication acts as another cornerstone, enabling partners to express their feelings, needs, and desires openly. As love's foundation strengthens through mutual understanding shared experiences, trust, and communication, it sets the stage for the growth of a lasting and resilient bond.

Nurturing the foundation of love requires ongoing effort and dedication. Acts of kindness respect, and support cement the emotional connection, helping it flourish even in the face of challenges. A willingness to compromise and a capacity to forgive and learn from mistakes are essential elements that fortify the foundation of love. Just as a sturdy structure requires maintenance, love demands continuous attention and care. Partners must remain attuned to each other's evolving needs and aspirations, adapting their behaviors and actions accordingly. As time passes the foundation of love can deepen and become more intricate, enriched by shared memories, growth, and the Intertwining of individual lives. In essence, the foundation of love is a dynamic and living entity that thrives on genuine emotions, mutual respect, unwavering support, and the endless pursuit of connection and understanding.

A. Understanding the Essence of Love

Understanding the essence of love is a complex and deeply philosophical endeavor that has captivated minds for centuries. At its core, love defies easy definition, transcending the boundaries of language and logic. It is an intricate interplay of emotions, actions, and connections that bind individuals together in a profound and often ineffable way. Love encompasses a myriad of forms, from the passionate and romantic to the nurturing and familial, making it a rich tapestry woven with diverse threads of human experience.

The essence of love extends beyond mere sentimentality. It embodies empathy, compassion, and a genuine concern for the well-being of another. It involves an acceptance of flaws and imperfections, and the willingness to support and uplift, even in the face of challenges. Love is an active force that requires effort, intention, and a willingness to truly see and understand another person. It flourishes in kindness, respect, and shared experiences, fostering a sense of unity that transcends the boundaries of individuality. To truly comprehend the essence of love is to embark on a lifelong journey of exploration, self-
8discovery, and connection with both oneself and the world at large.

B. Building a Strong Emotional Connection

Building a strong emotional connection is the cornerstone of a thriving and enduring marriage. It goes beyond mere companionship, encompassing a deep understanding and unwavering support for one another. Communication serves as the bedrock of this connection, fostering an environment where both partners feel heard, valued, and respected. Transparent and open conversations about hopes, dreams, fears, and even vulnerabilities lay the groundwork for intimacy. Sharing daily experiences, no matter how trivial, can create a sense of togetherness that weathers the storms of life. Moreover, empathy plays a pivotal role. Stepping into each other's shoes and genuinely comprehending each other's perspectives fosters a profound emotional bond. This connection acts as an emotional anchor, providing solace, joy. and a sense of belonging even amidst life's challenges, ultimately strengthening the marital bond.

Nurturing this connection also involves the practice of active appreciation and continuous effort. Expressing gratitude and acknowledging each other's efforts and qualities foster a positive atmosphere within the relationship. Regular date nights, shared hobbies, or even small gestures of affection help in keeping the spark alive. Both partners need to invest time and energy in understanding each other's evolving emotional needs and aspirations ensuring that the emotional connection remains a priority. Over the years, as life brings inevitable changes, maintaining this bond can serve as a resilient foundation,

offering unwavering emotional support and reaffirming the love that brought them together.

C. Effective Communication as the Cornerstone

Effective communication is the cornerstone of a thriving marriage, fostering a deep sense of understanding, connection, and intimacy between partners. At its core, successful communication in marriage involves both verbal and non-verbal exchanges that are characterized by active listening, empathy, and openness. Couples who engage in effective communication not only express their thoughts and feelings clearly but also take the time to truly comprehend their partner's perspective without judgment. This mutual respect of viewpoints creates an atmosphere of trust, where both individuals feel valued and validated.

In a marriage, effective communication goes beyond mere information exchange; it involves the ability to navigate conflicts and challenges with grace. Couples who communicate well are equipped to address disagreements constructively, steering clear of blame or criticism. Instead, they focus on using "I statements to express their emotions and needs. Therefore fostering a non-confrontational environment.

CHAPTER 2: CULTIVATING TRUST AND TRANSPARENCY

Cultivating trust and transparency forms the bedrock of a thriving marriage. Fostering an environment of emotional intimacy and mutual understanding. Trust, the cornerstone of any successful relationship, is nurtured through consistent honesty and reliability. Open communication about both triumphs and challenges creates a safe space for partners to share their thoughts, fears, and aspirations, fortifying the emotional connection between them. When Individuals feel confident that their partner's actions and words align, a sense of security takes foot, enabling them to weather life's storms as a united front Transparency, on the other hand, involves willingly revealing one's thoughts, emotions, and decisions to their spouse.

This practice engenders a deep sense of vulnerability that, paradoxically, strengthens the relationship. Sharing not only the positives but also the struggles and vulnerabilities foster an atmosphere of authenticity, enabling partners to truly understand each other's motivations and respond with empathy. Transparent communication helps prevent misunderstandings and assumptions, as both individuals are privy to the inner workings of each other's minds. As transparency becomes a habit, it erases the barriers that might otherwise lead to secrecy and resentment, promoting an enduring bond built on genuine emotional connection and shared experiences.

A. Fostering Trust Through Honesty and Transparency

Fostering trust through honesty and transparency is the cornerstone of building strong and enduring relationships, whether in personal interactions or within the realms of business and governance. Honesty serves as the foundation, setting the tone for open communication and mutual understanding. When individuals or organizations prioritize honesty, they demonstrate their commitment to integrity and ethical behavior. By sharing information truthfully, even when it might be uncomfortable or inconvenient, they create an environment where others feel valued and respected. This practice not only prevents misunderstandings but also allows for timely course corrections, bolstering collaboration and cooperation. When transparency accompanies honesty, showing a willingness to share information and decision-making processes openly, further solidifies trust.

This cultivates a sense of authenticity and reliability, reassuring stakeholders that there are no hidden agendas. Ultimately, the interplay of honesty and transparency forms a powerful bond that can weather challenges and nurture loyalty.

B. Respecting Individual Privacy within the Marriage

Respecting individual privacy within a marriage is paramount for maintaining trust, intimacy, and a healthy relationship. While marriage is a union of two individuals, it's important to recognize that each person still retains their autonomy and

personal boundaries. Open communication about privacy expectations, personal space, and the need for independent activities fosters understanding. Trust flourishes when both partners prioritize confidentiality. refrain from invading each other's personal spaces, and avoid prying into private matters without consent. This balance of togetherness and respect for individual privacy nurtures a strong foundation for a successful and harmonious marital bond.

C. The Power of Vulnerability in Strengthening Bonds

Vulnerability has the remarkable ability to forge unbreakable bonds within a marriage. When partners are willing to open themselves up and expose their true emotions, fears, and insecurities, they create an atmosphere of trust and intimacy that goes beyond the surface level. Sharing vulnerabilities requires an immense amount of courage and authenticity, demonstrating a deep commitment to the relationship.

In these moments of raw honesty, spouses often find themselves connecting on a much deeper level, as they recognize each other's humanity and imperfections. By showing vulnerability, individuals invite their partners to reciprocate, creating a reciprocal cycle of openness and understanding. This process not only fosters emotional closeness but also cultivates empathy and compassion, allowing couples to support each other through life's challenges with a profound sense of unity.

Moreover, vulnerability within a marriage encourages personal growth and development. As partners learn to communicate their vulnerabilities, they pave the way for constructive conversations about individual needs, boundaries, and aspirations. This open dialogue promotes a shared journey of self-discovery, where spouses can work together to overcome their weaknesses and build on their strengths. The mutual support that stems from embracing vulnerability allows couples to navigate hardships with resilience, emerging from difficult situations stronger than before. In turn, this mutual growth further solidifies the bond between partners, as they witness and facilitate each other's evolution. Ultimately, vulnerability catalyzes emotional intimacy and personal maturation, nurturing a profound and enduring connection in the institution of marriage.

CHAPTER 3: THE DANCE OF CONFLICT RESOLUTION

Conflict resolution in marriage is a cornerstone of maintaining a healthy and thriving relationship. In the journey of two individuals coming together, disagreements are inevitable due to differing perspectives, backgrounds, and needs. Effective conflict resolution involves a delicate balance between open communication, empathy, and compromise. Couples who excel in this skill often prioritize active listening, allowing each partner to express their feelings and concerns without fear of judgment. This not only fosters a deeper understanding of each 'other's viewpoints but also paves the way for finding common ground. Constructive discussions where both partners take responsibility for their feelings and actions lay the foundation for collaborative problem-solving. Instead of assigning blame, they focus on identifying the issue at hand and brainstorming solutions together. Ultimately, conflict resolution strengthens the emotional bond in marriage, demonstrating the mutual respect and commitment necessary for a lasting partnership.

Implementing effective conflict resolution strategies requires dedication and effort from both partners. It entails maintaining a sense of respect even in the heat of an argument and refraining from hurtful behaviors like name-calling or stonewalling. Taking breaks when needed can prevent discussions from escalating into shouting matches and provide individuals with the space to gather their thoughts. Moreover, practicing empathy plays a pivotal role in conflict resolution. Each partner should strive to understand the other's feelings and motivations, acknowledging that different life experiences
contribute to their perspectives. This empathy paves the way for compromise, where both individuals give and take to reach a resolution that considers both their needs. In essence, conflict resolution is not about eradicating disagreements but about navigating them in a way that strengthens the marital bond and helps both partners grow individually and as a couple.

A. Embracing Healthy Conflict as a Growth Opportunity

Embracing conflict as an opportunity for growth within a marriage can fundamentally transform the dynamics of the relationship. Rather than viewing conflicts as obstacles to be avoided, couples who approach disagreements as chances for deeper understanding and connection can foster an environment of emotional intimacy and resilience. When conflicts arise, they unveil differing perspectives, needs, and desires that might have remained hidden otherwise, By engaging in open and empathetic communication, partners can explore the underlying reasons behind their disagreements, leading to a more profound comprehension of each other's feelings and motivations. This process not only resolves immediate issues but also lays the groundwork for addressing future conflicts more constructively. Through active listening, compromise, and a commitment to mutual growth, couples can turn moments of tension into stepping stones toward a stronger and more harmonious partnership.

In this context, embracing conflict as an opportunity for growth involves a shift in mindset that encourages personal development alongside the evolution of the relationship. Each partner can reflect on their reactions and triggers, fostering self-awareness and personal growth. Moreover, the act of navigating disagreements together nurtures skills such as patience, empathy, and effective communication.

Over time, this practice creates a shared history of overcoming challenges and building a sense of shared accomplishment and trust. By acknowledging that conflicts are a natural part of any relationship and that they provide a chance to learn and adapt, couples can evolve in unison, deepening their bond while also becoming more resilient individuals. Ultimately, the journey of transforming conflicts into avenues for growth can be an enlightening and enriching aspect of a thriving marriage.

B. Active Listening and Empathetic Communication

Active listening and empathetic communication are two fundamental pillars of effective Interpersonal interactions. Active listening involves more than just hearing words; it requires giving the speaker your full attention, understanding their perspective, and responding thoughtfully, by focusing on the speaker's words, tone, and body language, active listening promotes deeper understanding and connection. This practice not only encourages the speaker to feel valued and heard but also helps the listener gather accurate information and context, leading to more meaningful conversations.

Empathetic communication complements active listening by acknowledging and understanding the emotions behind the words. It involves recognizing and sharing the feelings of others without judgment or offering solutions immediately. Empathy creates a safe space for individuals to express their thoughts and emotions openly, knowing that their feelings are validated and respected. This kind of communication fosters trust, compassion, and stronger relationships by demonstrating a genuine willingness to understand and support others on a deeper, emotional level. When combined, active listening and empathetic communication form a powerful duo that enhances understanding, empathy, and connection in various personal and professional contexts.

C. Negotiation and Compromise for Mutual Satisfaction

Negotiation and compromise serve as essential pillars for nurturing mutual satisfaction within a marriage. Every relationship inevitably encounters differences in opinions, preferences, and expectations. The art of negotiation involves open, honest, and empathetic communication where partners share their viewpoints without judgment. This practice encourages a deeper understanding of each other's needs and desires. Through constructive discussions, couples can work towards finding common ground and brainstorming solutions that accommodate both perspectives. This collaborative approach not only resolves conflicts but also strengthens the bond by showcasing a commitment to the relationship's well-being.

Complementing negotiation, compromise plays a crucial role in achieving mutual satisfaction. It requires a willingness from both partners to make concessions in certain areas to meet in the middle. Compromising involves letting go of rigid positions and finding solutions that blend aspects of both partners' wishes. This practice fosters an environment of teamwork and empathy, where each person's happiness is considered equally important. Skillful compromise demonstrates a dedication to the partnership's success and allows for a harmonious balance between individual needs and shared aspirations. Ultimately, the combination of negotiation and compromise paves the way for a resilient and contented marital relationship.

CHAPTER 4: INTIMACY AND ROMANCE

Intimacy and romance in marriage form the cornerstone of a deep and enduring connection between partners. Beyond the initial attraction, these elements thrive through shared moments, open communication, and a genuine understanding of each other's desires and vulnerabilities. Intimacy encompasses physical closeness as well as emotional vulnerability, allowing partners to express their true selves without fear of judgment. Romance, on the other hand, involves keeping the flame alive by fostering surprise, thoughtfulness, and continuous efforts to create special experiences. Nurturing intimacy and romance requires ongoing commitment, but the rewards of a strong marital bond built on these foundations are immeasurable, bringing couples closer and enhancing their shared journey through life.

Intimacy and romance are the threads that weave a tapestry of deep connection within a marriage. Intimacy goes beyond the physical, encompassing emotional vulnerability and trust that allow partners to share their hopes, fears, and dreams without reservation. It's about being each other's confidante, feeling secure in the warmth of companionship, and embracing one another's flaws and strengths. This emotional closeness fosters a sense of belonging and affirmation, nurturing a bond that strengthens over time.

Romance, on the other hand, injects excitement and passion into the everyday rhythm of married life. It involves creating
moments of delight and surprise, whether through thoughtful gestures, shared adventures, or reliving cherished memories. Sustaining romance requires effort and creativity, as partners continue to discover new ways to ignite the spark between them. From heartfelt conversations under the stars to spontaneous acts of kindness, these expressions of affection remind couples of the love that initially brought them together.

A. The Role of Emotional Intimacy in a fulfilling marriage

Emotional intimacy serves as a cornerstone of a deeply fulfilling relationship. It involves the mutual sharing of feelings, vulnerabilities, and experiences, fostering a profound sense of closeness and connection between partners. This level of intimacy creates an environment where individuals can be their authentic selves without fear of judgment leading to a strong bond built on trust and understanding. Through open communication, active listening, and empathy, emotional intimacy enables partners to provide unwavering support during challenging times and celebrate each other's joys. It deepens the emotional satisfaction within a relationship, enhancing not only the partners' connection but also their overall well-being.

Emotional intimacy is the invisible thread that weaves partners together in a fulfilling relationship. It goes beyond the surface and dives into the core of human connection, allowing individuals to share their deepest thoughts, fears, and dreams without reservation. This level of vulnerability creates a haven where both partners feel seen, heard, and accepted for who they truly are. The genuine understanding that stems from emotional intimacy nurtures a strong foundation of trust and empathy, enabling partners to navigate challenges hand in hand. In a fulfilling relationship, emotional intimacy acts as a nourishing foxier, continuously renewing the bond between partners. It fosters a profound sense of belonging and companionship, where each person's emotional needs are met and cherished. Through open conversations and active listening, partners build a treasure trove of shared experiences and memories that enhance their connection. This emotional doneness also leads to a

26

heightened sense of satisfaction and happiness, as partners derive immense support and comfort from their ability to connect on a deeper level.

B. Keeping the Spark Alive

Maintaining the spark in a relationship through creative romance involves infusing imagination and thoughtfulness into everyday Interactions. Surprise plays a pivotal role in planning unexpected romantic gestures, like a candlelit dinner at home or an impromptu picnic in the park, keeping the element of excitement alive. Creating personalized experiences, such as recreating a first date or revisiting significant places tap into nostalgia and remind partners of the journey they've shared.

Incorporating shared interests or exploring new ones together enhances the connection. Collaborating on a project, cooking a new recipe as a team, or even embarking on a spontaneous road trip fosters a sense of adventure and novelty. Engaging in playful activities, from board games to dance parties, brings out the inner child in both partners and strengthens the bond. The key is to keep reinventing how love and affection

are expressed, reminding each other of the deep emotions that initially sparked the relationship and fostering an enduring series of romance.

27

CHAPTER 5: ROLE AND RESPONSIBILITIES

Roles and responsibilities within a marriage are essential components that help foster a harmonious and functional partnership. While traditional gender roles have evolved, the key lies in establishing a dynamic that aligns with the couple's values, strengths, and preferences.

Open communication plays a pivotal role in defining these roles, allowing both partners to express their expectations, aspirations, and boundaries Modern marriages often emphasize equality, where responsibilities are divided based on individual skills; interests, and availability rather than predefined societal norms. This approach allows for a more balanced distribution of tasks, enabling each partner to contribute meaningfully to the relationship and the household.

In a successful marriage, responsibilities can encompass a wide range of areas, from financial management and child-rearing to household chores and emotional support. Flexibility is crucial, as life circumstances change over time. Both partners should be willing to adapt and recalibrate their roles as needed, taking into account factors like career shifts, health challenges, and personal growth. A strong partnership is built on collaboration, respect, and mutual appreciation for each other's contributions, regardless of whether they fit traditional gender roles or not. Ultimately, the key is to find a structure that aligns with the couple's shared vision and individual strengths. allowing them to navigate the complexities of life together.

A. Redefining Gender Roles in Modern Marriages

In modern marriages, there is a significant shift towards redefining traditional gender roles. Couples are increasingly recognizing the importance of equal partnership and shared responsibilities. Rather than conforming to predefined stereotypes, spouses are embracing a more fluid division of labor based on their individual strengths, preferences, and professional pursuits. This evolution in gender roles allows for greater flexibility in parenting. household management, and career ambitions. By challenging old norms, modern marriages foster open communication and mutual support, creating a more balanced and harmonious environment where both partners can thrive personally and professionally.

Redefining gender roles in modem marriages has become a dynamic and essential aspect of contemporary relationships. As society continues to progress towards greater gender equality, couples are actively reshaping traditional norms. In these partnerships, roles are no longer confined by expectations tied to one's gender. Instead, responsibilities are allocated based on individual strengths, interests, and availability. This shift has led to a more balanced distribution of tasks, whether they pertain to childcare, household chores, or career pursuits. The result is a partnership that emphasizes collaboration and communication, fostering an environment where both spouses can contribute meaningfully to all aspects of their shared life.

Moreover, the redefinition of gender roles in modern marriages has brought about benefits beyond the household. By transcending outdated conventions, couples are setting positive examples for future generations. Children raised in such environments witness the importance of mutual respect and cooperation. irrespective of gender. This reimagining of roles also extends to professional spheres, as couples actively support each other's ambitions and aspirations. Ultimately, the evolution of gender roles in modern marriages reflects society's progress toward a more inclusive and equal future, where relationships thrive on shared values and shared responsibilities.

B. Sharing Responsibilities Equitably

In a healthy and equitable marriage, sharing responsibilities is crucial to maintaining a balanced partnership. Both spouses contribute to various aspects of their shared life. such as household chores, financial decisions, childcare, and emotional support. Open communication and a willingness to understand each other's strengths and limitations help in determining how responsibilities are divided. This approach fosters a sense of teamwork, respect, and equality, allowing both partners to thrive individually while also nurturing their relationship together.

Equitably sharing responsibilities is the cornerstone of a successful and harmonious marriage. In this dynamic, both partners acknowledge each person's time, and energy. and abilities are valuable contributions to the partnership. By openly discussing and determining roles that align with their individual strengths and preferences, couples can distribute tasks such as household chores, financial management, and child-rearing fairly. This approach not only prevents the burden from falling disproportionately on one spouse but also cultivates a sense of mutual respect and cooperation. Moreover, an equitable distribution of responsibilities acknowledges the evolving nature of modern relationships. Partners recognize that traditional gender roles no longer dictate how tasks should be divided. Instead, they seek to strike a balance that honors their unique qualities and aspirations, promoting personal growth while strengthening the marital bond. Regular check-ins and adjustments to the arrangement ensure that both individuals feel supported, heard, and empowered, fostering an environment where each spouse's well-being and happiness are at the forefront.

C. Supporting Each Other's Personal and Professional Aspirations

In a marriage, supporting each other's personal and professional aspirations forms a strong foundation for mutual growth and happiness. When partners actively encourage and assist one another in pursuing their individual goals, it creates a sense of emotional closeness and understanding This support goes beyond just words, it involves actively listening, offering advice, and being present during challenges and triumphs. Whether it's pursuing a new career path, taking up a hobby, or embarking on a personal project, having a spouse who genuinely believes in your potential can provide the confidence needed to overcome obstacles.

Furthermore, supporting each other's professional aspirations can lead to a dynamic partnership where both individuals contribute their unique skills and talents to the relationship. It allows for the sharing of knowledge and experiences, fostering an environment of continuous learning. This collaborative approach can also bring a healthy balance to the marriage, as partners learn to manage their time effectively to accommodate both personal and joint goals. By prioritizing each other's aspirations, a couple not only enhances their individual growth but also strengthens their bond as they work together to build a fulfilling and purpose-driven life.

CHAPTER 6: GROWING TOGETHER AND INDIVIDUALLY

Marriage offers a unique and beautiful journey where two individuals embark on a shared path of growth while nurturing their own personal development. As partners, they face the joys and challenges of life side by side, fostering a deep connection that allows them to grow together. Through communication, compromise, and shared experiences, couples can develop a stronger bond that enables them to understand each other's strengths, weaknesses, and aspirations. This mutual growth strengthens the foundation of their relationship, helping them navigate life's twists and turns as a united force. Simultaneously, a healthy marriage recognizes the importance of individual growth within the context of togetherness. Each partner retains their unique identity, interests, and personal goals, enriching the relationship with diversity and individuality. By supporting each other's passions and giving space for personal exploration, spouses can encourage one another to become the best versions of themselves. This balance between growing together and individually in marriage ensures that the partnership remains dynamic, resilient, and full of opportunities for both partners to thrive.

In a strong and harmonious marriage, supporting each other's personal and professional aspirations becomes a cornerstone of mutual growth and happiness. Partners who celebrate and encourage one another's individual dreams create an environment where each person feels valued and understood. Whether it's pursuing a career milestone, embarking on a new hobby, or striving for personal development, the unwavering support from a spouse fosters a sense of emotional security and shared accomplishment. This collaborative approach not only strengthens the bond between partners but also sets an inspiring example for open communication, compromise, and a lifelong partnership dedicated to shared success.

A. Encouraging Personal Growth and Professional Aspiration

In a marriage, the act of supporting each other's personal and professional aspirations serves as a testament to the depth of commitment and love. When partners actively engage in the pursuits that bring joy and fulfillment to their spouse, a strong foundation of trust and companionship is built. This support isn't just limited to celebrating successes but also involves being a pillar of strength during setbacks and challenges.

Whether it's pursuing higher education, launching a new business venture, or exploring a passion, a partner's encouragement provides the motivation needed to overcome obstacles and reach new heights.

Moreover, this mutual encouragement in personal and professional endeavors not only empowers each individual to pursue their dreams but also cultivates an environment of shared growth. As partners cheer for one another's achievements, they create a sense of togetherness that extends beyond the confines of their own ambitions. This symbiotic relationship of support fosters open communication, empathy, and a profound understanding of each other's desires and goals. Ultimately, the intertwining of personal and professional aspirations in a marriage nurtures a bond that is not only strong and enduring but also continuously evolves through shared experiences and shared dreams.

B.Celebrating Each Other's Achievements and Milestones

Celebrating each other's achievements and milestones in a marriage is a cornerstone of nurturing a strong and enduring bond. It signifies a shared journey of growth, support, and unwavering commitment. In these moments of celebration, partners come together to acknowledge the individual strides they've made and the collective progress they've achieved. Whether it's a professional accomplishment, a personal triumph, or a mutual goal realized, taking the time to recognize and rejoice in these milestones helps foster a deep sense of mutual respect and admiration. Each celebration becomes a testament to the couple's shared joy, highlighting the belief in each other's potential and the genuine happiness found in seeing one another succeed.

Beyond the surface, celebrating achievements and milestones within a marriage also reinforces a sense of teamwork and solidarity. It involves embracing the highs and lows of life as a united front, standing side by side through every endeavor. By cheering for each other's victories, partners build a strong foundation of trust and emotional intimacy. This practice fosters an atmosphere of positivity and encouragement, creating a safe space where both individuals feel valued and validated. Ultimately, the act of celebrating each other's achievements in marriage strengthens the bond between partners, reminding them that they are not only companions on life's journey but also steadfast supporters of each other's dreams and aspirations.

C. Pursuing Individual Hobbies and Interests

Engaging in individual hobbies and interests is a vital avenue for personal growth and fulfillment. These pursuits provide a unique opportunity for individuals to explore their passions and express their creativity in ways that align with their preferences and inclinations. Whether it's painting, playing a musical instrument, coding, gardening, or any other endeavor, these hobbies offer an escape from the rigors of daily life and provide a sense of accomplishment that contributes to overall well-being. When people immerse themselves in their chosen hobbies, they enter a state of flow, where time seems to stand still and their focus is entirely on the task at hand. This not only leads to enhanced skill development but also serves as a form of relaxation, helping to reduce stress and boost mental parity. Furthermore, pursuing individual hobbies can foster a strong sense of identity and self-discovery.

Exploring one's interests allows for introspection and the opportunity to learn more about personal preferences, strengths, and weaknesses. Engaging in these activities can often lead to new friendships and connections with like-minded individuals who share similar passions. Moreover, hobbies often provide a balance to the routine of everyday life, infusing it with novelty and excitement. In a world where the demands of work and responsibilities can be overwhelming, carving out time for personal hobbies demonstrates a commitment to self-care and a recognition of the importance of nurturing one's own happiness. In essence, the pursuit of individual hobbies and interests contributes to a well-rounded and enriched life that goes beyond mere existence.

CHAPTER 7: WEATHERING LIFE'S STORMS

Marriage is a journey that often entails weathering life's storms together. Just as the weather can be unpredictable and challenging, couples often face unexpected trials and tribulations that test their bond. From financial struggles to personal setbacks, navigating these challenges as a team can fortify the relationship. Like a ship sailing through rough seas, couples who communicate openly support each other's growth and find solace in shared values, emerging from these storms even stronger. The experience of weathering life's ups and downs together fosters resilience, deepens understanding, and ultimately helps build a love that can withstand the tests of time.

In the intricate tapestry of marriage, the ability to weather life's storms together is a testament to the strength of the relationship. Just as a tree's roots grow deeper and stronger to withstand the force of wind and rain, couples face their own challenges that demand resilience and unity. From personal trials to external pressures, these storms can either erode the foundation or solidify the connection. It's in these moments that open communication becomes a lifeline, allowing partners to share their fears, hopes, and vulnerabilities. By leaning on each other's strengths and offering unwavering support, couples can find a way to navigate the tempests of life hand in hand, emerging with a deeper bond that has been tested and proven.

As time goes on, the storms that marriage encounters can come in various forms such as changing health issues, or even
differences in values. Each challenge presents an opportunity for growth and adaptation. Much like a lighthouse guiding ships through rough waters, shared values and mutual respect act as beacons that guide couples back to calmer shores. The journey of weathering these storms cultivates patience, empathy, and an understanding that the essence of marriage lies not just in the sunny days of joy but also in the steadfastness exhibited during the darkest of times. This shared experience knits hearts together, reminding couples of the unbreakable promise they made to support and cherish one another, no matter what life may bring.

A. Standing United in the Face of Challenges and Adversity

In the intricate journey of marriage, the concept of standing united gains paramount significance when faced with challenges and adversity. In times of difficulty, couples often discover the true strength of their bond as they navigate through the storm together. United, they form a formidable team that draws strength from their shared commitment. Challenges could arise from various forms such as financial strains, external pressures, or differences in opinion, yet the foundation of unity allows spouses to confront these obstacles with resilience. By standing united, couples create an atmosphere of unwavering support and open communication, which fosters a sense of togetherness that is crucial for weathering the storms that life inevitably brings.

The act of standing united in marriage isn't merely about weathering the tough times. It's also about reaping the rewards of shared triumphs. Overcoming challenges together can deepen the connection between partners, enhancing their understanding of each other's strengths and vulnerabilities. United, couples can channel their combined skills and perspectives to strategize, adapt, and find solutions. This unity empowers them to face adversity with a positive outlook, making their journey more fulfilling and sustainable. Moreover, by confronting challenges as a united front, couples set a powerful example for future hurdles, inspiring each other to remain steadfast while reinforcing their commitment to a shared life path.

B. Providing Unwavering Emotional Support

Unwavering emotional support forms the bedrock of a strong and lasting marriage. nurturing a deep connection that weathers life's challenges and celebrates its triumphs. It's a commitment to being there for one another, not just in times of joy, but also during moments of vulnerability and uncertainty. Providing unwavering emotional support involves active listening without judgment, offering a safe space for open communication, and a willingness to empathize with each other's experiences. This support is a constant reassurance that, no matter what, both partners have each other's backs.

CHAPTER 8: FAMILY AND PARENTING

Chapter 8 delves deeply into the intricate dynamics of family and parenting, highlighting the complex interplay of emotions, responsibilities, and connections that shape these essential aspects of human life. At its core, family serves as a foundation for nurturing and growth providing individuals with a sense of belonging and identity. The chapter discusses how families come in diverse forms, including nuclear families, extended families, single-parent households, and chosen families, each influencing the way individuals perceive themselves and the world around them Parenting, a central theme within this chapter, is explored as both a rewarding and challenging journey. The text emphasizes that effective parenting involves a delicate balance of nurturing and discipline, as caregivers strive to create a secure and supportive environment for their children's physical, emotional, and intellectual development. Moreover, the chapter underscores the importance of adapting parenting styles to each child's unique personality and needs, recognizing that there is no one-size-fits-all approach to raising children. It also addresses the evolving roles of parents in modern society, where shared responsibilities and open communication are increasingly valued.

The chapter also sheds light on the evolving concept of family in the context of broader societal changes. As norms and values shift, so too do traditional family structures, giving rise to discussions on topics such as co-parenting, and the impact of technology on family dynamics. The text encourages readers to reflect on their own family experiences, recognizing the strengths and challenges that arise within these relationships. Ultimately, this exploration of family and parenting serves as a reminder of the significance of these bonds in shaping individuals and society as a whole.

A. Navigating the Journey of Parenthood as a Team

Navigating the journey of parenthood as a team within a marriage is a profound and transformative experience that deepens the bonds between partners. As the couple transitions from being a duo to a family, their roles and responsibilities evolve, demanding a seamless synchronization of efforts. Effective communication forms the cornerstone of this collaborative approach. Sharing fears, aspirations, and practical concerns allows parents to create a united front, ensuring they can tackle challenges with a shared perspective. By openly discussing parenting philosophies, discipline strategies, and long-term goals, partners can align their values and create a harmonious environment for their children's growth. Flexibility and adaptability are essential attributes as couples venture into the uncharted territory of parenthood. Just as each child is unique, every stage of development brings new trials. Embracing change and adjusting expectations as circumstances evolve helps maintain equilibrium in the marriage. A strong support system is equally critical encouraging partners to take turns caring for the child, pursuing individual interests, and carving out quality time as a couple. This not only prevents burnout but also fosters a sense of autonomy within the marriage, nurturing personal growth alongside parental responsibilities. Amidst the whirlwind of diaper changes, sleepless nights, and school runs, it's vital for couples to nourish their emotional connection. Date nights, even if they occur at home, provide cherished opportunities to rekindle the romantic flame. Celebrating small victories and milestones together reinforces the sense of accomplishment and reinforces the team spirit. Parenthood tests patience, resilience, and empathy, qualities that, when nurtured as a team, not only enrich the parenting journey but mortify the marriage itself.

In weathering the storms and relishing the sunny days, couples discover that the shared endeavor of raising children hand in hand amplifies the joys and strengthens the love they share.

B. Balancing Family, Marriage and Self-care

Balancing the intricate dynamics of family, marriage, and self-care within the context of a marital relationship is a delicate art that requires conscious effort and thoughtful navigation. At the heart of this balancing act lies the recognition that both partners bring their unique needs, aspirations, and responsibilities to the union. Successful navigation of these aspects necessitates open communication and mutual understanding. Prioritizing family involves creating a supportive environment where communication forms the cornerstone of this collaborative approach. Sharing fears, aspirations, and practical concerns allows parents to create a united front, ensuring they can tackle challenges with a shared perspective. By openly discussing parenting philosophies, discipline strategies, and long-term goals, partners can align their values and create a harmonious environment for their children's growth.

Flexibility and adaptability are essential attributes as couples venture into the uncharted territory of parenthood. Just as each
child is unique, and every stage of development brings new trials. Embracing change and adjusting expectations as circumstances evolve helps maintain equilibrium in the marriage. A strong support system is equally critical encouraging partners to take turns caring for the child, pursuing individual interests, and carving out quality time as a couple. This not only prevents burnout but also fosters a sense of autonomy within the marriage, nurturing personal growth alongside parental responsibilities.

Amidst the whirlwind of diaper changes, sleepless nights, and school runs, it's vital for couples to nourish their emotional connection. Date nights, even if they occur at home, provide cherished opportunities to rekindle the romantic flame. Celebrating small victories and milestones together reinforces the sense of accomplishment and reinforces the team spirit. Parenthood tests patience, resilience, and empathy, qualities that, when nurtured as a team, not only enrich the parenting journey but fortify the marriage itself. In weathering the storms and relishing the sunny days, couples discover that the shared endeavor of raising children hand in hand amplifies" the joys and strengthens the love they share.

C. Instilling Values and Principles in the Next Generation

Instilling values and principles in the next generation is a pivotal responsibility that lays the foundation for a harmonious and ethical society. As elders, parents, educators, and mentors, it is our duty to guide the younger generation toward understanding the importance of values like empathy, integrity, respect, and responsibility. These values serve as a moral compass, helping Young individuals navigate life's complexities with a strong sense of right and wrong. By imparting these principles early on, we equip them with the tools to make informed decisions, contribute positively to their communities, and build meaningful relationships based on mutual trust and understanding. The process of instilling values and principles begins with setting a positive example. Children often emulate the behavior they observe, making it crucial for adults to model the values they wish to instill. Through open communication, discussions about real-life scenarios, and reflections on the consequences of actions, young minds can grasp the significance of ethical choices. It's essential to encourage critical thinking, enabling them to question, analyze, and discern the values presented in media, society, and their surroundings. By fostering a sense of autonomy in their value formation, we empower the next generation to develop a well-rounded ethical framework that can guide them throughout their lives.

In a rapidly changing world, instilling values and principles becomes even more vital as it provides a stabilizing force amid societal shifts. Teaching resilience, adaptability, and a commitment to core values prepares the next generation to face challenges with grace and determination. By emphasizing inclusivity, environmental stewardship, and a global perspective, we can nurture individuals who are not only responsible citizens but also compassionate global participants. Ultimately, the act of instilling values is an investment in the future, ensuring that the values we hold dear are carried forward to create a better world for generations to come.

In a marriage characterized by unwavering emotional support, spouses become each other's pillars of strength. They recognize the power of validation and encouragement, understanding that their partner's emotions and struggles are as significant as their own. Through life's ups and downs, they offer a steady and compassionate heart. Fostering an environment where both individuals can freely express themselves without fear of rejection. This deep sense of emotional security enables partiers to tackle challenges with newfound resilience knowing they are not alone in their journey. Ultimately, unwavering emotional support nurtures an atmosphere of love, trust, and, understanding, binding two people together in a bond that flourishes amidst life's unpredictable currents

CHAPTER 9: FRIENDSHIP AND COMPANIONSHIP

Friendship in marriage is a foundational bond that goes beyond the romantic connection. It involves a deep sense of companionship, trust, and mutual understanding between partners. When spouses share a strong friendship, they become each other's confidantes, offering unwavering support through life's ups and downs. This friendship creates a safe space where open communication thrives, allowing couples to discuss their thoughts, dreams, and concerns without fear of judgment. Laughter and shared interests also play a vital role, as friends within marriage often engage in activities that foster joy and create lasting memories. Nurturing friendship in marriage builds a resilient partnership, fostering a sense of partnership that endures challenges and celebrates victories together.

At the heart of friendship in marriage lies empathy and compassion. Partners who prioritize friendship cultivate an environment where they listen attentively and validate each other's feelings. This foundation enhances the emotional connection and encourages a willingness to compromise and find solutions to conflicts. Just as friends support one another's personal growth, friends within a marriage encourage each other to evolve and pursue individual aspirations. This balance of companionship and independence contributes to a fulfilling and enduring marital bond. In essence. friendship in marriage is a stone that enriches the partnership, making it more than just a union of two individuals, but a lifelong companionship brimming with understanding, camaraderie, and unwavering love.

Companionship forms the very foundation of a strong and fitting marriage goes beyond mere partnership and signifies a deep, emotional connection between two individuals. Companionship is the glue that binds couples together through life's ups and downs, fostering an adornment of understanding, empathy, and unwavering support. Companionship-based marriage, spouses become confident, sharing their dreams, fears, and aspirations without judgment. They engage in meaningful conversations, relishing each other's company and finding solace in the warmth of their togetherness. This level of companionship creates a safe space where both partners can be their authentic selves, allowing the relationship to evolve into a source of strength and comfort Companionship also paves the way for shared experiences and a sense of shared purpose, Couples who prioritize companionship actively partake in each other's Interests, hobbies, and activities, enriching their lives by creating lasting memories together. They become each other's go-to person for both celebrations and challenges. Finding joy in celebrating each other's successes, and finding strength in facing difficulties as a united front. As time goes on, the companionship deepens, resulting in a partnership that is not just built on love and attraction, but also on a profound friendship that sustains the marriage's longevity.

A.Treating Your Spouse as Your Best Friend

Being your spouse's best friend is a unique and profound bond that goes beyond romantic love. It's about sharing a deep connection built on trust, understanding, and unwavering support. As best friends, you're each other's confidants, able to
Share your joys, fears, and vulnerabilities without judgment. This level of emotional intimacy creates a safe space where you can be your true selves, fostering a sense of acceptance that strengthens your marital relationship. You engage in light-hearted banter, enjoy shared hobbies, and experience life's ups and downs side by side, creating a companionship that's enduring and comforting.

The foundation of a marital partnership rooted in the best friendship is communication. You listen to each other attentively, empathize with one another's challenges, and celebrate each other's victories as genuine cheerleaders. This friendship enhances the overall quality of your relationship, as you navigate life's challenges with a sense of camaraderie. From romantic gestures to inside jokes, you find joy in each other.

B. Laughing, Playing, and Exploring the World

In marriage, the shared experiences of laughter, play, and exploration create a strong foundation for a fulfilling and lasting bond. The ability to laugh together, whether it's over a funny movie, a silly inside joke, or just the quirks of everyday life, helps couples navigate challenges with resilience and positivity. Laughter fosters a sense of connection, easing tension and reminding partners of the joy in each other's company. It's a reminder that even in the face of difficulties, the ability to find humor can keep the relationship light-hearted and dynamic.

Playing and exploring the world as a team adds excitement to a marriage. Engaging in activities that bring out the inner child in both partners, such as board games, outdoor adventures, or even trying out new hobbies together can reignite the sense of curiosity and wonder that often gets overshadowed by adult responsibilities. Exploring new places, whether it's a foreign destination or a local hiking trail, allows couples to create shared memories and strengthens their sense of unity. Through these shared experiences, couples not only deepen their emotional connection but also create a reservoir of cherished

moments that contribute to the tapestry of their life journey together.

C. Creating Shared Memories and Traditions

Creating shared memories and traditions is a cornerstone of a strong and lasting marriage. These experiences serve as the foundation upon which couples build their unique story, fostering a sense of unity and connection. From celebrating milestones like anniversaries to simple everyday rituals, shared memories help partners navigate challenges and celebrate joys together. Whether it's a yearly vacation spot, a special date night, or a cherished inside joke, these moments form a tapestry that reflects the journey of the relationship. By intentionally cultivating such memories, couples forge a deep emotional bond that strengthens their commitment over time.

Traditions, on the other hand, provide a roadmap for couples to navigate their married life. These can range from cooking a favorite meal together every Sunday to attending cultural events as a family. Establishing traditions not only creates a sense of predictability and comfort but also fosters a sense of identity within the marriage. Through these practices, partners blend their individual backgrounds and preferences, crafting a new shared culture that helps sustain their connection in times of change embarked upon.

CHAPTER 10: SUSTAINING LONG-TERM PASSION

Long-term passion marriages require a dedicated mindful spark. Attraction and infatuation may naturally cultivate deeper and enduring relationships through various means. Understanding each other's changing preferences, regularly expressing appreciation, shared dreams, thoughts, and intimacy reignites the flame. Couples should prioritize spending quality time together that both enjoy and that they connect deeper with new hobbies, going on romantic getaways, and fostering cherished memories that deepen their emotional connection.

Individual identities within the marriage are essential. Pursuing interests only enriches partners and also brings new continuously evolving individuals. The evolving dynamics of a long-term relationship is a journey that communication, empathy, and a willingness to embrace change. Relationships naturally grow and evolve, which leads to prioritizing, and goal-setting. This necessitates ongoing support of one another's changing needs. Regular honest aspirations and individual growth help bridge a deeper connection built on mutual respect.

Flexibility is a cornerstone of navigating the changing tides of a long-term relationship. Just as life itself is dynamic, so too are the circumstances that impact a partnership. Adapting requires letting go of rigidity and finding new ways to engage, explore shared interests, and create fresh experiences together. The ability to compromise and find common ground becomes even

more crucial enabling both partners to maintain their sense of identity while also fostering the unity that comes with shared goals. Adapting to evolving dynamics isn't about avoiding challenges but rather about facing them together, recognizing that the growth of the relationship is an ongoing collaborative effort.

A.Keeping the Relationship Exciting and Fresh

Keeping a marriage exciting and fresh requires consistent effort and a willingness to evolve together. One key aspect is maintaining open communication, regularly sharing thoughts, dreams, and even concerns helps keep the emotional connection strong. It's also important to actively listen and show empathy toward each other's feelings. By Continuously understanding each other's changing needs, couples can adapt and grow in sync.

Variety and novelty play a crucial role in preventing monotony. Engaging in new activities together, whether it's trying a new hobby, traveling to unfamiliar places, or even experimenting with different cuisines, injects a sense of adventure into the relationship. Planning surprise date nights or weekend getaways can add an element of unpredictability and keep the romance alive. At the same time, nurturing individuality within the partnership is equally vital. Allowing each other space to pursue personal interests fosters a sense of independence, which can in turn rekindle excitement when sharing those experiences with one another.

B. Embracing Change in a Marital Relationship

Embracing change while holding on to what truly matters is a delicate art in the context of marriage. Relationships inevitably evolve over time influenced by various factors such as personal growth, external circumstances, and shifting priorities. It's crucial for couples to acknowledge that change is a natural part of life's journey and to approach it with open hearts. This might involve adapting to new roles, interests, or responsibilities that come with different life stages. However, amidst these shifts, it's essential to retain a strong connection to the core values, shared experiences, and emotional intimacy that formed the foundation of the relationship.

Communication becomes a powerful tool in navigating change within a marriage. Open and honest conversations about individual aspirations, collective goals, and mutual expectations can foster understanding and unity. As partners embrace change together. they can actively choose to prioritize the aspects that truly matter. This might involve setting aside time for quality moments, practicing empathy, and continuing to show appreciation for one another. By holding onto the values and principles that brought them together in the first place, while remaining adaptable to the dynamic nature of life, couples can strengthen their bond and create a resilient partnership that thrives amidst change.

CHAPTER 11: THE POWER OF FORGIVENESS

The power of forgiveness in marriage is a transformative force that can mend wounds, strengthen bonds, and nurture lasting love in the intricate dance of a marital relationship. Conflicts and misunderstandings are inevitable. It's in these moments that forgiveness takes center stage. When partners choose to forgive each other's mistakes, they demonstrate not only empathy and compassion but also a deep commitment to the relationship's growth. Forgiveness allows couples to move beyond resentment and bitterness, creating space for healing and renewal. By letting go of grudges, spouses can rebuild trust and create an environment where open communication and vulnerability can flourish. It's through forgiveness that couples learn to appreciate each other's imperfections and work together to overcome challenges, ultimately forging a more resilient and harmonious union.

However, forgiveness in marriage doesn't imply turning a blind eye to recurring issues or accepting harmful behavior. Instead, it's a deliberate choice to acknowledge the pain, address the root causes, and actively work towards reconciliation. It requires genuine effort from both partners to seek understanding, apologize, and make amends. The power of forgiveness lies not only in its ability to heal the past but also in its capacity to shape the future of the relationship. As couples learn to forgive and be forgiven, they foster an environment of emotional safety and mutual respect. This, in turn, lays the foundation for a marriage that thrives on mutual growth, deep connection, and unwavering support.

A. Understanding the Healing Nature of Forgiveness

Understanding the healing nature of forgiveness unveils the transformative power it holds in mending emotional wounds and fostering personal growth. Forgiveness doesn't merely entail pardoning the actions of others. It's an internal process that liberates the forgiver from the clutches of resentment, anger, and pain. By choosing to forgive, individuals release themselves from the burden of negative emotions, allowing space for healing and renewal. This act of compassion and empathy paves the way for emotional liberation, enabling one to move forward with a lighter heart and a renewed perspective.

Forgiveness not only benefits the forgiver but also contributes to the broader fabric of relationships and communities. When we extend forgiveness, we break the cycle of negativity and resentment, fostering an environment of understanding and empathy. It has the power to rebuild broken connections, offering an opportunity for reconciliation and growth. The healing nature of forgiveness lies in its ability to reshape perspectives. promote emotional well-being, and ultimately, contribute to the creation of a more harmonious and interconnected world.

B. Understanding Empathy in a Marital Relationship

Empathy is the cornerstone of healthy and meaningful relationships, demonstrating a genuine understanding and concern for another person's emotions and experiences. One of the primary ways a person shows empathy in a relationship is through active listening. This involves giving their full attention to the other person, suspending judgment, and truly absorbing what they're saying. By validating the other person's feelings and thoughts, whether they're expressing joy, sorrow, frustration, or anxiety, an empathetic individual creates a safe space for open communication.

Furthermore, someone displaying empathy in a relationship takes the time to put themselves in the other person's shoes. This involves imagining how they would feel in a similar situation, allowing them to better comprehend the emotional landscape their partner is navigating. By doing so, they can respond with compassion and understanding addressing the other person's needs and concerns in a way that aligns with their emotions. This empathetic perspective fosters a deeper connection and fosters a sense of mutual support.

Lastly, an empathetic person demonstrates their care through actions. They actively engage in acts of kindness and consideration going out of their way to provide comfort and support when needed. Whether it's preparing a favorite meal, offering a shoulder to cry on, or helping with tasks during a tough time, these gestures communicate their sincere investment in the other person's well-being. By consistently demonstrating empathy through both words and actions, they establish a strong foundation of trust, closeness, and understanding within the relationship.

C. Letting Go of Grudges and Resentment

Letting go of grudges and resentment is of paramount importance for our emotional well-being and personal growth. Carrying these negative emotions can weigh us down, impacting our mental health and relationships. When we hold onto grudges, we continually relive past hurts, preventing us from moving forward and finding peace. The constant replaying of negative experiences can lead to stress, anxiety, and even physical health problems. By releasing these negative feelings, we free ourselves from the shackles of the past and create space for positivity in our lives. Furthermore, letting go of grudges fosters healthier relationships and facilitates personal growth. Holding onto resentment often keeps us stuck in a cycle of conflict, preventing us from fostering meaningful connections with others. By forgiving and moving on, we open the door to empathy, understanding, and effective communication. Moreover, the act of letting go reflects our own emotional maturity and inner strength. It allows us to focus on our own personal development and invest our energy in constructive endeavors rather than dwelling on negativity. In the end, releasing grudges and resentment is an essential step towards achieving emotional freedom and building a more fulfilling life.

D. Rebuilding Trust After Transgression

Rebuilding trust after transgressions is a delicate and gradual process that demands commitment, empathy, and open communication.When trust has been damaged, acknowledging
the wrongdoing is the first step. Taking responsibility for one's actions and showing genuine remorse helps demonstrate accountability. Alongside this, an honest explanation of what happened and why it occurred can provide the affected parties with clarity and understanding, fostering an environment where both sides can work toward resolution. Patience becomes essential, as rebuilding trust requires time. Consistent and reliable behavior over an extended period of time can gradually repair the fractured trust, indicating a genuine commitment to change Throughout this journey, active listening and empathy, are vital components. Openly discussing feelings, concerns, and expectations allows for a deeper understanding of each other's perspectives. Encouraging the expression of emotions, even if they are uncomfortable, helps in validating the hurt party's experience and ensures that their feelings are acknowledged. Establishing clear boundaries, and mutual agreements, and moving forward are crucial to preventing similar transgressions and rebuilding a stronger foundation of trust. Ultimately, the process of rebuilding trust after

transgressions demands vulnerability, dedication, and a shared willingness to mend what has been broken.

CHAPTER 12: CULTIVATING GRATITUDE

Chapter 12 delves into the profound significance of cultivating gratitude in our lives. Gratitude serves as a powerful lens through which we can appreciate the positives amidst challenges. By actively acknowledging and expressing thanks for the blessings we have, we shift our focus from what we lack to what we possess. This shift in perspective can lead to enhanced mental well-being and emotional resilience, helping us cope with stress and adversity more effectively. Moreover, practicing gratitude fosters stronger interpersonal connections, as expressing gratitude not only uplifts our own spirits but also reinforces bonds with others. This chapter explores how embracing gratitude as a daily habit can ultimately promote a more positive and fulfilling life experience. in a world often driven by constant striving and comparison, cultivating gratitude offers a counterbalance. It reminds us to pause and recognize the simple pleasures and accomplishments that enrich our lives. This practice can temper feelings of entitlement and dissatisfaction, fostering contentment with the present moment. Furthermore, the cultivation of gratitude extends beyond individual benefits. It can create a ripple effect in our communities, inspiring acts of kindness and compassion. By acknowledging the contributions of others and expressing our appreciation, we foster an atmosphere of mutual support and collaboration. As Chapter 12 emphasizes, cultivating gratitude is not just a personal endeavor, but a transformative force that can positively influence our inner selves and the world around us.

A. Recognizing and Appreciating Each other's Effort

Recognizing and appreciating each other's efforts is a fundamental aspect of building strong relationships and fostering a positive environment. When individuals acknowledge the hard work and contributions of others, it not only boosts morale but also cultivates a sense of validation and value. This recognition serves as a powerful motivator, encouraging individuals to continue investing their time and energy into their tasks. By expressing appreciation, people demonstrate empathy and respect, creating a supportive atmosphere that encourages collaboration and teamwork.

Furthermore, recognizing and appreciating efforts can lead to improved communication and reduced misunderstandings. When people feel valued, they are more likely to openly share their ideas and concerns, leading to a more transparent exchange of thoughts. This, in turn, enhances problem-solving and decision-making processes, as team members feel comfortable discussing their perspectives. Overall, fostering a culture of recognition and appreciation creates a harmonious environment where individuals feel acknowledged, motivated, and connected, ultimately contributing to higher levels of productivity and satisfaction.

B. Expressing Gratitude as a Daily Practice

In the journey of marriage, the practice of expressing gratitude on a daily basis holds a profound significance. It acts as a
nurturing force, fostering an atmosphere of appreciation and mutual understanding. Regularly acknowledging the small gestures, thoughtful actions, and even the routine support provided by one's partner can cultivate a deep sense of connection. Gratitude serves as a reminder of the positive aspects of the relationship, which can be especially crucial during challenging times. By consistently expressing gratitude, couples can create a foundation of positivity, helping them navigate through conflicts and differences with empathy and respect.

Furthermore, the act of showing gratitude in a marriage goes beyond mere words it demonstrates a genuine acknowledgment of one another's efforts. It validates the emotional investments each partner makes, reinforcing a sense of being seen and valued. As partners continually express gratitude, it becomes a habit that shapes their perception of the relationship. This practice not only bolsters marital satisfaction but also encourages ongoing acts of kindness and consideration. In essence, the daily expression of gratitude becomes a transformative tool that strengthens the bond between spouses, allowing them to grow both as individuals and as a united partnership.

C. Fostering Positivity and Contentment in the Relationship

In the intricate tapestry of a marital relationship, fostering positivity and contentment is akin to nourishing the roots of a flourishing tree. It forms the cornerstone of a strong and lasting bond, providing the emotional sustenance needed to weather the inevitable storms of life. When positivity becomes a shared value, partners tend to approach challenges as a united front, rather than adversaries. This cultivates an atmosphere of mutual respect and understanding, allowing them to communicate openly and empathetically. The ripple effect of positive interactions extends beyond just the couple, influencing the overall family dynamics and even individual well-being. Contentment, on the other hand, acts as a compass, guiding partners to cherish and celebrate the present rather than endlessly seeking fulfillment elsewhere. When both individuals prioritize finding joy within their relationship, they create a harmonious space where love and companionship can thrive.

Neglecting positivity and contentment, however, can lead to the erosion of the marital foundation. Constant negativity can create a toxic environment, eroding trust and erasing the emotional safety that a healthy relationship requires. Without a counterthreat, the relationship can fall prey to a perpetual cycle of dissatisfaction, breeding resentment and potentially pushing partners apart. Struggles and conflicts are inevitable, but a foundation of positivity and contentment helps couples navigate these challenges with grace and resilience. In nurturing these qualities, couples equip themselves with the slopes needed to build a lasting connection that not only survives but also flourishes over time.

CONCLUSION: SUMMING IT ALL UP

A lifetime of love is a remarkable journey that transcends time and challenges, weaving a tapestry of emotions, experiences, and connections. It is a story of commitment, resilience, and shared growth. Through the ups and downs, the laughter and tears, love remains a constant force, guiding individuals through the various stages of life. The initial spark of infatuation evolves into a deep and profound connection, rooted in understanding and acceptance. As the years pass, love matures, adapting to the changing circumstances and evolving into a steadfast companionship that nurtures and supports both partners.

In the tapestry of a lifetime of love, milestones, and memories are woven with threads of affection and trust. The journey is not without its challenges, but it's the commitment to weathering storms together that strengthens the bond. Each passing day becomes a testament to the enduring power of love, as partners become each other's pillars of strength, sources of joy, and unwavering support. A lifetime of love is not merely about the passage of time but about the quality of moments shared and the depth of connection forged. It's a journey that leaves an indelible mark on the hearts of those who embark upon it, reminding us of the beauty of human connection and the capacity for love to enrich our lives beyond measure.

A. REFLECTING ON THE JOURNEY OF A HEALTHY MARRIAGE

A journey of a healthy marriage is akin to embarking on a lifelong adventure, filled with twists, turns, and breathtaking landscapes. As couples reflect on this transformative journey, they often find themselves marveling at the growth they've experienced both individually and together. In the initial stages, the excitement of new love and shared dreams sets the tone, igniting the flames of passion. But as time marches on, the relationship evolves into a profound partnership, where companionship and understanding become the cornerstones of a solid foundation.

Throughout the journey, challenges are inevitable. It's during these moments of adversity that a healthy marriage truly shines. Partners learn to navigate storms with open communication, unwavering support, and a shared commitment to weathering any hardships together. Reflecting on these challenges allows couples to recognize the strength of their bond, celebrating the resilience that has carried them through the toughest of times. Just as a tree's roots grow stronger when faced with powerful winds, marriage becomes more unbreakable when tested by life's trials.

The journey of a healthy marriage is a tapestry woven with countless threads of shared experiences, mutual growth, and cherished memories. Reflecting on this journey evokes a sense of gratitude for the countless small moments that have shaped the relationship's trajectory. From simple acts of kindness to grand gestures of love, each stitch in the fabric of their journey contributes to a beautiful mosaic of a life well lived together.

Ultimately, this reflection reinforces the profound truth that a healthy marriage is not a destination but an ongoing expedition, where the partners continue to discover new facets of themselves, their relationship, and the limitless potential of their love.

B. Continuously Working on the Relationship's Growth

Continuously working on the growth of a marital relationship is akin to nurturing a delicate plant. Just as a plant requires consistent care, attention, and nurturing to flourish, so does a marriage that demands ongoing effort and dedication to thrive. It's a dynamic journey that involves mutual respect, communication, and a shared commitment to personal and joint development. The path to a resilient and thriving marital bond requires partners to be attuned to each other's evolving needs and aspirations, fostering an environment where both individuals can flourish.

in the realm of marital growth, communication stands as the cornerstone. Regular and open dialogue provides the opportunity to share thoughts, concerns, and dreams, thereby fostering a deeper understanding of one another. Engaging in active listening and empathetic communication nurtures a sense of validation and emotional intimacy, reinforcing the foundation of trust. As individuals evolve, the relationship must adapt accordingly. This might involve setting joint goals, supporting each other's aspirations, and finding ways to navigate challenges together. The commitment to growing together, even through difficulties, lays the groundwork for a partnership that not only endures but thrives.

Just like a garden requires regular tending to keep it free from weeds, a marital relationship demands ongoing effort to weed out negative patterns or behaviors that can hinder growth. Partners must be attuned to their emotional well-being and that of their spouse, offering support and encouragement where needed. This might involve seeking external guidance, such as therapy or counseling, to address deeper issues constructively. Through these shared experiences, couples can learn to celebrate their triumphs and learn from their setbacks, creating a sense of unity that reinforces their connection. Ultimately, the journey of continually nurturing a marital relationship's growth is a testament to the power of love, commitment, and the human capacity to evolve harmoniously over time.

BOOKS AVAILABLE BY THE SAME AUTHOR
THE FIRST AMERICANS A CHILDREN'S BOOK FOR
AGES 8 TO 12
A SPIRITUAL GUIDE TO EMOTIONAL MATURITY
IN ROMANTIC AND MARITAL RELATIONSHIPS
106

BERMUDA TRIANGLE MYSTERY

FOR KIDS

CHARLES MCKINNEY

DR. HISTORY

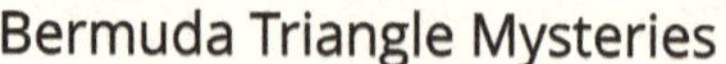

BERMUDA TRIANGLE MYSTERIES

The Dreaded Bermuda Triangle: Strange and Amazing Facts and Myths

FOR KIDS

CHARLES MCKINNEY

DR. HISTORY

Don't Forget Your Free Bonus Downloads!

As our way of saying thank you, we've included in every purchase bonus gift downloads. If you've enjoyed reading this book, please consider leaving a review.

Or Scan Your Phone to open QR code

Bermuda Triangle Mysteries:

The Dreaded Bermuda Triangle: Strange and Amazing Facts and Myths

Copyright © 2023 by Dr. History

TABLE OF CONTENTS

INTRODUCTION

Full fathom five thy father lies. Of his bones are coral made; Those are pearls that were his eyes; Nothing of him that doth fade But doth suffer a sea-change Into something rich and strange. (I.ii.) Ariel's words. The Tempest

by William Shakespeare.

Legend has it that the shipwreck scene from Shakespeare's fascinating drama, The Tempest, is based on other texts of the time describing the strange disappearances of vessels in that stretch of the Atlantic Ocean roughly triangled by Miami, Puerto Rico, and Bermuda called the Bermuda Triangle.

The Bermuda Triangle is a place of strange happenings. Dozens of airplanes and ships have disappeared there for completely unexplained reasons. There have been ships disappearing without trace or distress signal, even in fair weather. A squadron of US navy bombers disappeared without a trace. Let's examine the strange circumstances of the flights and vessels that disappeared without a trace and decide which side you support.

Skeptics say that the Bermuda Triangle is all about myth and hype and that aircraft and vessels have regularly and mysteriously disappeared from other well-traveled sections of the ocean. They insist that people traverse that area safely on a daily basis.

Many people believe that the Bermuda Triangle is the Devil's Triangle. Even the explorer Christopher Columbus noted a flaming object falling into the sea and scores of unexplained events. Many paranormal authors have suggested that the Triangle's lethality stems from things as diverse as Atlantis, aliens, sea monsters, reverse gravity fields, and time warps. Scientifically minded believers in the Bermuda Triangle have suggested magnetic aberrations, waterspouts, or enormous methane eruptions from the ocean floor. What we do know for sure is that approximately 50 ships and at least 20 airplanes have gone down since people began noticing the phenomenon.

The question we need to ask ourselves is not only why this happened but what the significance is if, indeed, there is any significance. We'll do this by examining the geography of the area and the various incidents that have occurred and then have a good look at the Science and the Mythology behind the Bermuda Triangle before deciding whether we're on the side of fact or fiction.

THE BERMUDA TRIANGLE

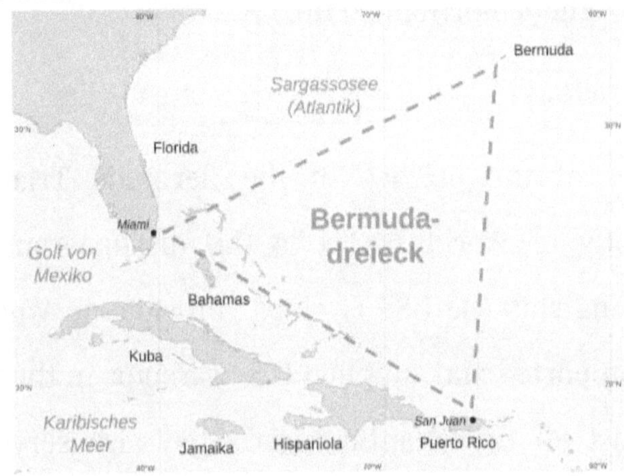

The Bermuda Triangle is a place of strange happenings. Dozens of airplanes and ships have disappeared there for completely unexplained reasons. There have been ships disappearing without trace or distress signal, even in fair weather. A squadron of US navy bombers disappeared without a trace.

The region called Bermuda or Devil's Triangle encompasses approximately 500,000 square miles of sea off the southeast tip of Florida. When the great explorer Christopher Columbus traveled through the region on his first great expedition to the Americas, which he called the New World, he noted that an enormous fiery flame (possibly a meteor) smashed into the ocean one evening and that an odd glow occurred in the distance some weeks later. He furthermore put down that there were unpredictable readings from his ship's compass. This is possible because, at that time, a fraction of the Bermuda

Triangle was one of the isolated places on the Globe where the true and magnetic north lined up.

The USS Cyclops

Another of the puzzles of the Bermuda Triangle and, consequently of World War I is the disappearance of the coal-carrying ship the USS Cyclops. Previous to World War I, the ship supported and supplied U.S. warships in the waters of Europe, just off the Atlantic coast. They also served in the Caribbean as a squadron of the Naval Auxiliary Force. Early in March 1918, while they were returning from a journey to Brazil somewhere between Barbados and Chesapeake Bay, the Cyclops vanished with all crew on board. Although she was fitted to do so, she never sent out an SOS call. Many boats sailed to find her as she was believed to have been destroyed by a German submarine. The wreck of the 542-foot-long ship with more than 300 men and 10,000 tons of ore onboard plunged somewhere into the Ocean. Many people credited her disappearance to the Bermuda Triangle, especially when, in 1941, two of her sister ships disappeared without a trace along a similar route.

Joshua Slocum: After gaining extensive prestige as the first individual to sail solo around the world, Joshua Slocum vanished, with his boat The Spray, without a trace on a voyage from Martha's Vineyard to South America in 1909. Though it's uncertain what occurred, many sources later credited his loss to the mysterious Bermuda Triangle. Speculation was rife as to the cause as he was a family man and a fine sailor. Possibly one of the violent and sudden storms in the Bermuda Triangle caused his demise. Or possibly it was something more mysterious.

Joshua Slocum

After gaining extensive prestige as the first individual to sail solo around the world, Joshua Slocum vanished, with his boat, The Spray, without a trace on a voyage from Martha's Vineyard to South America in 1909. Though it's uncertain what occurred, many sources later credited his loss to the mysterious Bermuda Triangle. Speculation was rife as to the cause as he was a family man and a fine sailor. One of the violent and sudden storms in the Bermuda Triangle possibly caused his dcmise. Or possibly it was something more mysterious.

The Navy Bombers

A pattern was beginning to form in which boats or planes crossing the Bermuda Triangle would either vanish or be found with no souls aboard. In 1945, in December, five Navy bomber planes crewed by 14 men left Fort Lauderdale, Florida, to practice bombing over some convenient shoals of fish. The mission leader, whose compass was seemingly malfunctioning, got extremely lost. All five aircraft flew erratically until they ran out of fuel and were compelled to land in the Sea. That very day, a recovery plane and its crew also vanished. After a vast search of some weeks did not find any evidence, and they were declared lost. Flight 19 disappeared over the Bermuda Triangle. The weather was thought to have turned nasty, and the men were trainee pilots, but no wreckage or evidence was found.

Amelia Earhart and Turkish Airlines A330-200

The famous Amelia Earhart, the first woman to fly solo across the Atlantic, was also lost over the ocean. Her final flight in January 1939 was considered to have come down in the Bermuda Triangle.

In a more modern example, in 2017, a Turkish Airlines A330-200 airbus suffered a succession of mechanical and electrical faults while flying over the Triangle. They were forced to re-route, fortunately avoiding disaster.

The famous Amelia Earhart, the first woman to successfully do a cross-Atlantic solo flight, was lost over the ocean too. Her final flight in January 1939 was thought to have come down in the Bermuda Triangle. She was never found.

Other Lost Souls

On November 3, 1978, Eastern Caribbean Airways Flight 912, due to land at St. Thomas disappeared even after having been glimpsed by the control tower. No trace of her was ever found.

In June 2005, a small plane, a Piper PA-23, vanished somewhere between Treasure Cay Island in the Bahamas and Fort Pierce in Florida. All three souls on board were lost.

On April 10, 2007, another Piper light plane vanished near Bird Cay. It had flown into a severe thunderstorm and lost altitude. Two people died.

On May 15, 2017, a private aircraft was at 24,000 ft when it disappeared from the radar and contacted the air traffic control in Miami. Some wreckage from the plane was later found.

As recently as December 2, 2022, an Air France airliner suffered several electronic problems with its media systems and the failure of an anti-icing component that ultimately forced the airplane to return to its starting point in Martinique.

This and other less well-documented examples have led to the speculation that the Bermuda triangle might be a cursed area. Let's look at the possible reasons behind these disasters.

Fun Fact:

William Shakespeare's drama "The Tempest," some scholars of literature and history assert, was based on a genuine Bermuda shipwreck. This may have strengthened the region's mysterious aura. However, rumors and reports of mysterious disappearances only captured the public's attention after the 20th century. This is possible because of improved communication.

Fun Fact:

A small section of the Bermuda Triangle is noteworthy for being one of only two areas on Earth where the compass indicates true north instead of magnetic north as it does in most places. If the pilot is inexperienced or distracted, this compass deviation might not be compensated for, and vessels and aircraft might unexpectedly find themselves far from their planned course.

Which of these statements are thought to be True or False?

1. William Shakespeare's The Tempest was thought to be based on a shipwreck in the Bermuda Triangle.

2. Only magnetic North can be read in the Bermuda Triangle.

3. Experienced pilots crewed the Navy bombers in 1945.

4. Vasco da Gama saw a fiery object fall into the sea thought to be within the Bermuda Triangle.

5. In 2022, an Air France plane had to turn back from the Bermuda Triangle because of technical issues.

6. The famous Amelia Earhart, the first woman to fly solo across the Atlantic, was also lost over the ocean.

7. The USS Cyclops was a warship.

8. Three hundred men were lost from the USS Cyclops.

Answers:

1. True

2. False. This is one of the few places on the globe where the compass indicates true and magnetic north.

3. False. Trainee pilots crewed the Navy bombers.

4. False. It was Christopher Columbus.

5. True.

6. True

7. False. It was a cargo ship.

8. True.

WHAT WE KNOW AND DON'T KNOW ABOUT THE BERMUDA TRIANGLE

It's interesting to examine the facts we know about the Bermuda Triangle and juxtapose them against the "facts" that might just be suppositions.

The Facts

1. The Bermuda Triangle is a broad area roughly in the North Atlantic Ocean. It is edged by the southeastern shores of Bermuda, the U.S., and the Greater Antilles Islands, including Jamaica, Cuba, Puerto Rico, and Hispaniola.

2. While the precise boundaries of the Triangle are not agreed on by all, the approximate area ranges between 1,300,000 and 3,900,000 square kilometers or 500,000 and 1,510,000 square miles. The area has an imaginary triangular shape.

3. The Bermuda Triangle does not occur on any map of the

globe and is not recognized by authorities as an official or even accepted area of the Atlantic Ocean.

4. Although statements of mysterious incidents in the area are dated to the mid-1800s, the term "Bermuda Triangle" was only found after 1964. The term first occurred in print in a popular magazine, in an article by Vincent Gaddis. Gaddis employed the phrase to define a triangular-shaped region "that has destroyed hundreds of ships and planes without a trace."

5. Despite its formidable reputation, the number of incidences in the Bermuda Triangle is relatively low. There are comparable disappearances in other regions of the Atlantic Ocean.

6. As described in Section 1, two incidents, at least the USS Cyclops and the Flight 19 bombers, involved craft belonging to the US military.

7. The best-selling book by Charles Berlitz, The Bermuda Triangle, written in 1974, popularized the mythology behind the Bermuda Triangle. In this story, Berlitz contended that a mythological lost island called Atlantis

was somehow involved in the disappearance of these crafts.

8. In 2013, The World Wildlife Fund completed a comprehensive survey of all ocean shipping lanes and deduced that the Bermuda Triangle is not included in the earth's 10 most hazardous stretches of ocean for shipping.

9. The Bermuda Triangle has unusually heavy daily traffic by sea and air and is one of the most highly traversed shipping lanes on the globe.

10. The agonic line occasionally goes through the Bermuda Triangle. This happened for an interval in the early 1900s. The agonic line is an area on the Earth's surface where magnetic north and true north line up, and there is no necessity for mariners and pilots to take account of this difference on the compass.

11. The Bermuda Triangle is prone to regular, severe tropical hurricanes and storms.

12. The Gulf Stream, a powerful maritime current known to result in quick local weather changes, goes through the

Bermuda Triangle.

13. The deepest place in the Atlantic Ocean, called the Milwaukee Depth, is found in the Bermuda Triangle. The deepest section is the Puerto Rico Trench which has a depth of 8,380 meters or 27,493 feet.

What we don't know about the Bermuda Triangle

1. There is no record of the precise number of airplanes and vessels that have vanished in the Bermuda Triangle. The most widespread estimate is 20 airplanes and 50 ships.

2. Unusually, the wrecks of many of the ships and airplanes noted as missing in the area have never been recovered.

3. It is not certain whether these disappearances of vessels and planes in the Bermuda Triangle result from severe weather, other phenomena, or human error.

Certainly, while a great deal is known about the Bermuda Triangle, many questions remain unanswered. Unexplained factors surround certain of these disasters. A good example is the squadron of Navy bombers who mysteriously became disoriented while in transit over the area. Even stranger is the number of boats and planes that have vanished in clear weather.

The experts largely agree that there is no significant danger or risk in traveling across the Bermuda Triangle, while the conspiracy theories and other fanciful souls insist on a myriad of highly imaginative theories. Many, many vessels and planes cross the area daily without incident but in the back of one's mind remains the niggly little question about what happened to those who did not make safe passage. This is what keeps the mystery of the Bermuda Triangle alive. And so the speculation continues unabated.

And the mystery continues!

Fun Fact:

The Bermuda Triangle is thought by many to be a paranormal site in which the unchangeable laws of physics are inexplicably damaged or altered. Despite the common refusal of the United States Coast Guard, scientists, and others to give credence to these speculations, the assessment of such paranormal activity continues.

Fun Fact:

The Agonic line is an imaginary line on the earth's surface. This connects the magnetic poles from the north and the south. When one passes through these points, there is no magnetic declination. A magnetic needle, freely suspended, will indicate true north. Inexperienced navigators might not realize the significance of this phenomenon.

Fill in the blanks to complete the story.

Other ______ and airplanes apparently have ______ from the region in favorable weather without even reading in ______ messages. But although ______ frivolous theories have been suggested regarding the Bermuda Triangle, none substantiate that mysterious ______ happen more often there than in other______ areas. In fact, people navigate the region every day without ______.

Answers:

Other **boats** and airplanes apparently have **vanished** from the region in favorable weather without even reading in **distress** messages. But although **myriad** frivolous theories have been suggested regarding the Bermuda Triangle, none substantiate that mysterious **disappearances** happen more often there than in other **well-traveled** ocean areas. In fact, people navigate the region every day without **incident.**

THE KRAKEN AWAKES

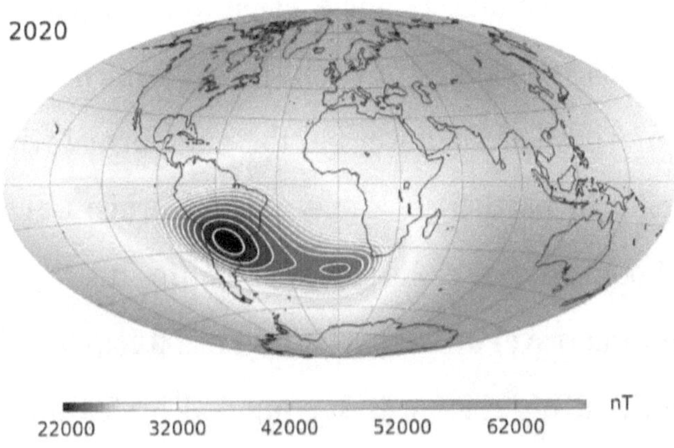

The South Atlantic Anomaly: Also known as the SAA, (the outer space Bermuda Triangle) is an unexpectedly weak place in the Earth's magnetic field. Unfortunately, it seems to be growing and dividing into two sections. For people on Earth, the SAA generates no apparent harm at ground level but in space, this anomaly behaves like a "pothole" for spacecraft and satellites.

Many people believe the popular legend that the Bermuda Triangle is the Devil's Triangle.

Paranormal writers have implied that the triangle's deadliness arises from elements as diverse as wormholes, Atlantis, Aliens, and Sea monsters.

Wormholes, Atlantis, Aliens, Sea monsters

Let's look at some fanciful theories.

Wormholes, Reverse Gravity Fields, and Time Warps

Could the Bermuda Triangle cause one to leap ahead in time and space? Could it even be a leap into a fourth dimension? There are believers in the paranormal who believe so. One pilot in particular, a man named Bruce Gernon, who wrote a book on his experiences, had this to say "I didn't believe in time travel or teleportation until it happened to me," He alleged that his craft was surrounded by fog and then he leaped 100 miles ahead. Maybe all those ships and planes ended up in another dimension!

Atlantis

Charles Berlitz of The Bermuda Triangle fame came up with the notion that the lost city of Atlantis was in some way accountable for the plane crashes and shipwrecks in the Bermuda Triangle. Since then, other theorists have jumped on the bandwagon, contending that technology invented by Atlanteans, including crystal energy, remains active on the seabed, resulting in mechanical malfunction in the boats and planes above that part of the ocean. However, the main flaw in this hypothesis is that there's no proof that Atlantis ever existed.

Aliens

There's no surprise in this theory. Wherever conspiracy theorists exist, there are always UFOs. In this situation, the tale goes that alien beings use the Bermuda Triangle as a doorway to planet Earth. There predictably, they collect the humans and technology they require to perform research on the human species. This theory clarifies why so many ships and airplanes lost in the Bermuda Triangle are never found again, even as wreckage.

Sea Monsters

For those with really vivid imaginations, the huge sea monster, a giant squid called a Kraken, could drag ships, and low-flying planes down into the depths with it, ostensibly to feast upon the tender flesh of their inmates. Now that's really pushing it!

Scientific Theories

Scientifically minded supporters of the Bermuda Triangle have proposed that water spouts, magnetic anomalies, or enormous methane eruptions on the Ocean Floor are responsible. They've thrown in some rogue waves for good measure so let's start with them.

Rogue Waves

A rogue wave is an excessively large and unpredictable surge of water, commonly twice as high as the other waves surrounding it. Some years ago, scientists at Southampton University in the UK alleged that the water of the Bermuda Triangle was particularly prone to rogue waves owing to storms that move in from four sides. Some of these waves, the researchers suggested, could be 100 feet high. While the work of these scientists' received a great deal of scrutiny, they could not solve the mystery of what would cause a plane crash in the Bermuda Triangle.

Magnetic Forces

As explained previously, the Bermuda Triangle is one of two spots on Earth where a navigator's compass will reflect true instead of magnetic north. While true north is a fixed juncture where the lines of longitude meet up on a map, magnetic north continually shifts as it's the place on the surface of the Earth where the magnetic field points directly in a downward direction. The discrepancy between the magnetic and true north is called "declination," and all well-trained vessel and airplane navigators know to chart their courses correctly, bearing this in mind. The assumption is that inexperienced pilots didn't realize this and got horribly lost and disappeared. Seems unlikely.

Methane Bubbles

A group of Norwegian researchers in 2016 claimed that they had found huge, half-mile craters in the sea bottom off the coast of Norway. According to their hypothesis, the craters were created by unexpected explosions from very deep methane deposits below the sea. This created a stir as people tried to extrapolate this theory to explain the marine accidents in the Bermuda Triangle.

Waterspouts

According to scientists at NASA, waterspouts are spiraling columns of damp air formed over warm ocean water. Like ocean tornadoes, waterspouts can have wind speeds of up to an intense 125 miles per hour. Because the Atlantic Ocean off the Florida coast is a hazardous weather area, some people have speculated that they might have caused the Bermuda Triangle catastrophes. According to Scientists, this theory might be closest to the truth. Severe weather could definitely be complicated in the Triangle losses.

So we're no wiser about the actual cause of these mysterious losses.

Fun Fact:

There is also the "Sargasso Sea Theory." The Sargasso Sea, named after Sargassum, a variety of seaweed that fills the region's waters, is the only sea with no beaches or coastlines. Although it's not bounded by land, it is distinguished by four sea currents. Some people believe that where these ocean currents meet, they trap ships in a certain way so they can not move, falter, and sink.

Fun Fact:

The Kraken, from the fascinating world of Greek Mythology, is reputedly a sea monster of enormous size and unbelievable strength. It was created from a match between Oceanus and Ceto, Titans who were sea entities. Its tentacles are vast enough to haul entire ships beneath the water and even demolish cities without any difficulty.

Reflection Question:

The Australian scientist Karl Kruszelnicki, who researched the Bermuda Triangle, proclaimed that the lost vessels and planes were nothing but "human error, bad weather, heavy air, and sea traffic." The distrustful scientist contended that the elevated number of vessels and planes lost was not supernatural but merely an unfortunate series of circumstances.

That's his opinion. If you were to play Devil's advocate and argue with him, which of the reasons in Section 3 for the Triangle tragedies would you choose? **Substantiate your answer.**

HOW RISKY IS TRAVELING ACROSS THE BERMUDA TRIANGLE?

Planes, Ships, and People Have All Disappeared without a Trace: Skeptics say that the Bermuda Triangle is all about myth and hype and that aircraft and vessels have regularly and mysteriously disappeared from other well-traveled sections of the ocean. They insist that people traverse that area safely on a daily basis. There are many people, however, who believe that the Bermuda Triangle is the Devil's Triangle. Even the explorer Christopher Columbus noted a flaming object falling into the sea there and there have been scores of unexplained. events.

Ask the Triangle Theorists

In the 1964 Pulp Magazine article, Vincent Geddis named the area where three crafts had just disappeared after sending "all's well" messages to the Bermuda Triangle. Paranormal guru Charles Berlitz began researching the topic and writing a fascinating and fanciful book about it. When Berlitz published his best-selling book The Bermuda Triangle, which incidentally sold in excess of 14 million copies, it created enormous hype around the Bermuda Triangle.

The Risks

Naturally, mariners, pilots, and their passengers wanted to know what chance they had of vanishing forever into a watery grave. In reality, though, there is no one theory that unravels the Bermuda mystery. As one cynic put it, attempting to find a predominant cause for every Bermuda Triangle disaster is less logical than finding a common reason for every car accident in any given city.

Also, although hurricanes, reefs, and the unpredictable Gulf Stream can result in nautical challenges in that area, maritime insurers Lloyd's of London do not acknowledge the Bermuda Triangle as a particularly dangerous place. In the words of the U.S. Coast Guard, "nothing has been discovered that would indicate that casualties were the result of anything other than physical causes. No extraordinary factors have ever been identified." The area also has extremely high sea and air travel levels, most of which pass through unscathed.

The Reasons

These high numbers of incidents could then be attributed to the huge percentage of traffic that travels through this area. It is an important shipping lane between the US's East Coast and the Gulf of Mexico, and, particularly recently, it has become a busy route for aircraft too.

So what's caused the disasters? According to the authorities, weather conditions appear to be the obvious explanation. It is a very prominent area for hurricanes to move through. The island of Bermuda stands in what is called Hurricane alley, the favored route of Atlantic Hurricanes. It's therefore unsurprising that the old-fashioned systems of planes and ships without new weather radar techniques might come into this area and be shocked by some terrible and unexpected storms.

Add to this the magnetism theory with which we're now familiar. Your inexperienced or ignorant navigators could be pushed way off course by thinking they were heading for magnetic north when their compasses indicated true north. Particularly in the pre-GPS days, when navigators depended on their compasses and the stars (if the weather permitted but not very likely in the heart of a storm), they would have tried to correct from Magnetic to True, but doing that along an agonic line would certainly have steered them into trouble.

Another problem is the deep trenches in this region of the sea. Most of the seabed is as deep as 27,500 feet. This means that when boats and planes sink in that area, they are not easy to find. This creates the temptation to suspect wormholes and aliens.

Sad to say, for the Triangle Theorists, bad weather and high traffic seem to be the main risk to traveling across the Bermuda Triangle.

Fun Fact:

If one reads through the catalog of air and sea incidents and disasters pertaining to the Bermuda Triangle, it's interesting to note that most incidents happened in the mid-1900s. The exceptions were the strange incidents affecting Turkish Airlines TK183 and a few accidents affecting light aircraft.

Fun Fact:

One of the biggest mysteries of all, Flight 19 has been attributed to the inexperienced pilot and flight leader confusing the Bahamas and the Florida Keys, a damaged compass, and the regrettable advice given to the squadron that if they lost themselves in the region, they should just "take up a heading of 270."

Fill In the Blanks to Complete the Story

The lack of recent _________ incidents attributable to _________ manifestations does suggest that it was presumably due to more _________ reasons that incidents were higher here than in other _________. Added to the fact that it makes a good _________, we find we just have an area of bad _________, lots of _________, and disappointingly _________ reasons for disasters.

(Aviation, unexciting, supernatural, traffic, standard, weather, areas, story)

Answer:

The lack of recent **aviation** incidents attributable to **supernatural** manifestations does suggest that it was presumably due to more **standard** reasons that incidents were higher here than in other **areas**. Added to the fact that it makes a good **story**, we find we just have an area of bad **weather**, lots of **traffic**, and disappointingly **unexciting** reasons for disasters.

ANOTHER BERMUDA TRIANGLE THE DRAGON'S TRIANGLE

There are lots of strange and bizarre places around the earth on both land and sea that are almost impossible to understand logically. The tales of lost vessels and ghost ships wandering aimlessly without being crewed in these areas have made them synonymous with mystery.

Though the famous Bermuda triangle tops the list of most frightening places on this earth, a number of other locales also prevail as almost as mysterious as the former. The Devil's Sea also called the Dragon's Triangle, is another nightmare for sailors.

The Devil's Triangle

Situated near the coast of Japan in the Pacific Ocean is the Devil's Sea. This is called Ma-no Umi in Japanese. It is one of twelve "Vile Vortices" found around the planet. Vile vortices are regions where the force of the planet's electromagnetic waves is stronger than anywhere else. The Dragon's Triangle is a triangle between the Islands of Bonin and Japan and includes a major part of the Philippine Sea.

Geographically, this triangle is found near Miyake, a Japanese island a hundred kilometers south of Tokyo. Although the actual spot is hotly debated, particularly since it's not recorded on a map.

The region has also been named the "Pacific Bermuda Triangle" for a while its position is opposite to the Bermuda Triangle, and the resemblances in the strange phenomena are the same as those of the Bermuda Triangle.

Reports of mysterious occurrences date back into history, but there have been many unexplained reports of ships vanishing. According to legend, the oceans of the triangle are infamous for making even the most robust vessels vanish with all hands on board.

Noteworthy incidents in the Devil's Sea

It is said that the great conqueror Kublai Khan, grandson of Genghis Khan, had attempted to invade Japan in 1274 and 1281 AD. However, both times, he failed to raid the country after his boats, and 40,000 crew were lost in this area because of hurricanes. The Japanese concluded that their gods sent the storms to save them. Marine archaeologists have subsequently found the remains of the Mongol fleets.

Another tale tells of the sighting of a strange woman sailing a boat in the Devil's triangle in the early 19th century. It is said that the boat looked like a traditional Japanese Incense burner. The identity of the craft and where it was headed remains a mystery.

In the 1940s and 50s, some fishing and five military boats disappeared into the sea in the region between Iwo Jima and Miyake Island. Japan dispatched a research vessel, the Kaio Maru, in 1952 to investigate these lost boats, but this vessel, too, with 31 crew, vanished. The wreck of the boat was found later, but all signs of the crew had disappeared.

After this incident, the government of Japan proclaimed this area hazardous for marine travel. They did not pursue any further attempts to discover the mystery. However, popular myths believe that undersea dragons come to the surface to sate their hunger, hence the name Dragon's Triangle.

Fun Fact:

A scholar called Ivan Sanderson has indicated that the combination of hot and cold currents which cross the Vile Vortice led to the vanishing of boats in this Devil's Sea. After studying the area, he suggests that these currents caused electromagnetic disruptions that entrapped the passing ships and caused them to sink.

Fun Fact:

Another theory suggests that undersea volcanoes in this region caused the vessels to disappear. The eruptions from such volcanoes could have caused these accidents, corroborating the tales of underwater dragons sucking boats and crew to their death. Apparently, islands also disappear, and others reappear in different areas.

True or False:

1. A Vile Vortice has unusually high electromagnetic currents.

2. These are 13 Vile Vortices in the world that are sinister.

3. A boat shaped like an incense burner was seen in the 1800s.

4. The Mongol Empire defeated the Triangle and invaded Japan.

5. The Japanese Government disputed any mystery in the Region.

6. Dragons do live under the Ocean.

7. Undersea volcanoes might have caused the ships to sink.

8. Islands sink and rise in this area.

Answers:

1. A Vile Vortice has unusually high electromagnetic currents. **True**

2. These are 13 Vile Vortices in the world that are sinister. **False. There are only 12.**

3. A boat shaped like an incense burner was seen in the 1800s. **True.**

4. The Mongol Empire defeated the Triangle and invaded Japan. **False. They sank into the Devil's Sea.**

5. The Japanese Government disputed any mystery in the Region. **False. They found it unsafe to travel.**

6. Dragons do live under the Ocean. **False. Dragons don't exist.**

7. Undersea volcanoes might have caused the ships to sink. **True.**

8. Islands sink and rise in this area. **True.**

THE OUTER SPACE BERMUDA TRIANGLE

I bet you didn't know that a Bermuda Triangle exists in outer space.

Interestingly enough, astronauts have a "Bermuda Triangle" of their very own to deal with. It's situated right over the South Pacific and stretches between Zimbabwe and Chile. It's also a great deal more convincing than its counterpart on Earth. It's called the South Atlantic Anomaly, and while, in this situation, nobody is alleging that craft is unexpectedly disappearing, the disturbance that's being generated is nonetheless significant, and it poses great difficulties for both devices and astronauts because high quantities of radiation affect the spacecraft's electronic networks.

To explain this phenomenon, Earth has two of these Van Allen belts, a pair of doughnut-shaped bands of charged atomic particles that encircle our planet, held firmly in place by the planet's magnetic field. The inner part comprises primarily high-energy protons, and the outer area comprises mainly electrons. Because the belts capture the particles that are shooting away from the sun's surface, they protect the surface of the earth from destructive radiation

In a nutshell, these rings of electrically charged particles have high numbers of electrons in the outer circle and highly energized protons in the inner circle surrounding the Earth. The Earth's magnetic field produces these, and they protect life on earth from dangerous radiation by trapping radioactive atoms in its magnetic hold.

Unfortunately, in this specific area, the magnetic field surrounding the earth is quite weak, so those atomic particles are unrestricted and can move around a great deal more than in other areas. Also, they have succeeded in getting much nearer to Earth, implying that our space equipment, satellites, and astronauts occasionally orbit through it. This pretty much messes with electrical equipment and people, for that matter.

It's important to note that the Hubble telescope, which passes through the outer space Bermuda Triangle at least ten times a day, has its workings disturbed for at least 15% of every day. Satellites also often encounter short-term system failures when they pass through on days of high flux. The astronauts on the International Space Station must be safeguarded to deter excessive exposure to radiation. The astronauts often report glimpsing spontaneous white flashes and have regular issues with their communication devices.

The Hubble telescope is particularly important, which is why the aberrations from the South Atlantic Anomaly are so annoying. Hubble's observations have, over the years, enabled scientists to determine the expansion of the universe, spot Pluto's moons, and give mankind the pleasure of seeing strange, as yet unidentified worlds. One of the most exciting things Hubble recently found was the furthest star called Earendel. The pictures portray Earendel as it had been 12.9 billion years ago. (That's only 900 million years after the world began with the Big Bang, for those who subscribe to that theory.)

One can see that these strange Bermuda and other aberrant triangles can be a real nuisance, but they also show us that man is a tiny blip in a fascinating natural world.

Fun Fact:

The South Atlantic Anomaly or SAA (the outer space Bermuda Triangle) is unexpectedly weak in the Earth's magnetic field. Unfortunately, it seems to be growing and dividing into two sections. For people on Earth, the SAA generates no apparent harm at ground level, but in space, this anomaly behaves like a "pothole" for spacecraft and satellites.

Fun Fact:

Over recent years, the South Atlantic Anomaly has been to blame for various spacecraft failures and even rules when or when not astronauts can conduct their spacewalks. As space close to Earth becomes filled with increasing numbers of spacecraft, there are questions about the future safety of spaceflight.

Trivia Questions:

1. What's the name of the outer space Bermuda Triangle?
2. What important scientific tool is affected by this Triangle?
3. What's the name of the atom belts that protect the Earth?
4. What do they protect the Earth from?
5. What has the furthest star been called?

Answers:

1. The South Atlantic Anomaly.

2. The Hubble Telescope.

3. The Van Allen Belts.

4. Radiation from the Sun.

5. Earendel.

BERMUDA. A SKEPTIC'S OPINION

In his article, "Bermuda Triangle: Where Facts Disappear," published in 2012, Benjamin Radford, investigator, and eminent writer, debunks much of the information thought to be "fact" about the Bermuda Triangle.

Debunking the theories (and the theories.)

Bradford begins by questioning some popular hype about a Bermuda Triangle connection with the Malaysian airline flight MH 370, even though it crashed half a world away from the Bermuda Triangle. He expressed very scathing views on the gullibility of the general public.

He mentions that the term "Bermuda Triangle " was given to the area in 1964 by the writer Vincent Gaddis in Argosy, the pulp magazine Argosy and describes the contribution of Charles Berlitz, who wrote the bestselling 1974 "non-fiction" book "The Bermuda Triangle," with scorn, belittling the theories that have fascinated the world.

Radford questions how the lost city of Atlantis, should it even exist, would somehow sink ships using crystal energies. He speculated why time portals, rips in space's fabric, should suddenly open over that particular area or where extraterrestrials kept their imaginary underwater bases while waiting to capture unwary earthlings.

Radford rips apart the theory of methane bubbles with his satirical musings on the coincidence of a methane bubble appearing next to a ship and being ignited, possibly by a lightning bolt, to create the massive explosion that would sink a ship or blow a plane out of the sky. He commented dryly that methane exists across the globe and does not affect areas so dramatically.

Radford even mocks the notion that pilots would get confused by the geomagnetic anomaly caused by the confusion between true and magnetic north, questioning that while one might imagine pilots losing control and plunging into the sea, it doesn't explain ships. He quotes the official position of the Naval authorities, which is that while such an anomaly had existed in the 1800s, the fluctuating magnetic field has altered, meaning that the situation had not existed for 100 years or more.

Is there actually any mystery about the Bermuda Triangle?

Radford suggests that before accepting any of the above explanations, a true skeptic or discerning scientist should inquire with a more fundamental question: Is there actually any mystery to clarify?

Larry Kusche, a journalist, agreed with him by asking that same question and coming up with the answer that there is no mystery, in fact, about odd Bermuda Triangle disappearances Kusche comprehensively re-examined the "mysterious disappearances" and established that the stories were basically built in blunders, mystery mongering, and certain cases, outright fraudulent lies all being ratified as valid checked facts. He was particularly critical of Charles Berlitz, calling his work "sloppy" and full of "unscientific crank theories." He claimed that ships reported lost never existed or sank far from the Bermuda Triangle or "mysteriously" during severe storms.

Sometimes, no concrete evidence suggests that ships and

planes have vanished in the "aquatic triangular graveyard." These occurrences were purported to have originated from a writer's imagination. But when the vessels involved did exist, Berlitz and others failed to reiterate that they "mysteriously disappeared" during severe weather disturbances. Other times, the ships sank far from the Bermuda Triangle territory.

Radford noted the region within the Bermuda Triangle because it is heavily traveled, with both passenger and cargo ships; logically, not randomly would be expected to have more boats disappear there than in less well-traveled areas.

Fun Fact:

Major conspiracy theories are frequently hard to refute. Look at the Covid-19 vaccine theories! Some may include bits of truth or nourish an emotional need in their believers. And hardcore conspiracy supporters are gifted at rationalizing away information that negates their beliefs. Could this be the case with the Bermuda Triangle?

Fun Fact:

What about one of the biggest conspiracy theories of its time? We know that in 1969 astronauts landed on the moon. By the 1970s, though, a bizarre conspiracy theory had emerged. It claimed that the moon landing never occurred. This conspiracy was narrated in a 1976 self-published book, "We Never Went to the Moon: America's Thirty Billion Dollar Swindle," and received uncanny support.

Fill in the missing words below from this quote by Benjamin Radford

"In the end, there's no need to __________ time portals, __________, submerged ___ bases, geomagnetic __________, tidal waves, or anything else. The Bermuda Triangle __________ has a simpler explanation: __________ research and __________, mystery-__________ books."

(Atlantis, UFO, invoke, sloppy, sensational, anomalies, mongering, sensational.)

Answers:

"In the end, there's no need to **invoke** time portals, **Atlantis**, submerged **UFO** bases, geomagnetic **anomalies**, tidal waves, or anything else. The Bermuda Triangle **mystery** has a simpler explanation: **sloppy** research and **sensational**, mystery-**mongering** books."

BERMUDA TRIANGLE REAL OR NOT? WHAT DOES THE MAN IN THE STREET THINK?

Well, whether or not the US coast guard, scientists, investigative journalists, and other well-qualified people think, the average man in the street tends to disagree. It's pretty obvious that people prefer a mystery to a boring explanation like storm damage. A survey of people's opinions about the real reasons behind the Bermuda mysteries is pretty bizarre.

Let the people speak.

1. If boats and ships are wooden, I don't see how they would be affected by a magnetic field, so it can't be that!

2. Our generation has been created for about seven thousand years. Before we arrived, there were other races who were destroyed. We don't know if they all disappeared or if some were hijacked into outer space and want to come back in UFOs. It's quite possible that extraterrestrials are involved.

3. Why not circles instead of triangles? Something to do

with earth's ley lines?

4. The ships vanish through portals into other dimensions.

5. The triangle has a hidden Island in the middle, and all the planes and boats are stored there.

6. Some things are beyond human understanding. God made a mysterious world.

7. A group of sharks is eating all the people. That's why they can't be found.

8. I often ask myself why there are things that look as if they were made by humans living underwater. I don't have a conclusive answer, but I hypothesize that other humans before us lived in the ocean. Our answers lie in the "Mariana Trench." We know that he saved a man after the great flood, but what about those people he didn't save? Maybe vestiges of them will live underwater. They build things underwater that we build on earth.

9. What about air bombs? These are hexagon-shaped holes in the clouds. It's quite logical to think that if they hit a ship, plane, or the water around it, it would cause a sinking.

10. There's a beast called Leviathan. It says so in the Bible.

11. In Ancient times, operations involving gravity fields went wrong on Atlantis, and efforts to amend the situation were ineffective. One moon crashed down where the Bermuda Triangle was followed by the other, which crashed into the Dragon's Triangle, and both resulted in dimensional doors! That is also how we ended up with only one moon. Mind-blowing! These entities visit us in the current day. I have glimpsed their vehicles myself.

12. The Bermuda Triangle is dangerous, and I recommend people stay far away.

13. The Bermuda Triangle is the most outstanding magical place in the world. It's like area 51 and Chernobyl, where many people have asserted that they have seen the strange phenomenon.

14. Even though I don't believe the Bermuda Triangle is malicious, I certainly would not seek out a direct path through it.

The words of people speak for themselves. Whether or not the Bermuda Triangle is sinister, most people want it to be.

Since Atlantis seems to be high on everyone's belief system, here are a couple of fun facts about it.

Fun Fact:

According to the Greek philosopher Plato, the utopian kingdom, situated on an Island, was in existence some 9,000 years before his day and mysteriously vanished one day. The city was famed for being the seat of all earthly pleasures. Sounds inviting! Plato saw Atlantas as the role model for his fabled "Republic."

Fun Fact:

The Atlanteans apparently had exceptional energies, possibly because many think they were a colony of Mars so they would have had supernatural abilities. They were thought to be able to modify volcanic activity and take control of the weather. Just like the Greek gods! Maybe that is where Plato got the idea, or maybe he knew something we don't.

Discussion Question:

You have heard the scientific evidence. You've had some access to public opinion. So what's your opinion? Is the Bermuda Triangle a serious phenomenon or just a string of coincidences? What do you think has caused those Vessels and Planes to disappear? Justify your answer.

YOUR BERMUDA TRIANGLE EXPERIENCE

The Tempest- William Shakespeare's drama "The Tempest," some scholars of literature and history assert was based on a genuine Bermuda shipwreck. This may have strengthened the region's mysterious aura. However, rumors and reports of mysterious disappearances only captured the public's attention after the 20th century. This is possible because of improved communication.

You can immerse yourself in the Bermuda Triangle Hype in many ways through books, novels and nonfiction, documentaries and horror movies, or even for the very adventurous, a Bermuda Triangle cruise.

The Books

An interesting book, written along the lines of Charles

Berlitz, famous Gian Quasar, wrote a controversial study in 2005 called "Into the Bermuda Triangle: Pursuing the Truth Behind the World's Greatest Mystery."

This book promises us that it's in pursuit of the truth.

It draws on official documents from the NTSB and other agencies investigating mysteries and consultations with theorists, scientists, and survivors. It documents the range of disappearances of planes and ships over the Bermuda Triangle, exploring possible rationales ranging from magnetic vortices to zero-point energy.

The mysteries of the Bermuda Triangle are still unsolved, still perplexing, and taking new victims. The book promises some untold stories.

- An airplane pilot notices a strange haze surrounding his plane, then he vanishes eleven hours after reaching fuel starvation as if shouting out from a chasm; his voice is heard 600 miles from where he should have been. He asks for authorization to land, then disappears forever.
- A sea freight vessel steaming over tranquil seas vanishes without a trace.

- A leisure sailboat ghosts past without a person on board.

- A plane pilot calls for assistance because a "weird object" is persecuting his plane.

- A jet collides with an "unknown" entity and is never seen again.

This is a must-read for readers who can't get enough of the Bermuda Triangle.

A Movie

There is no shortage of Bermuda Triangle movies (feels like nearly one a year,) but this one released in 2009 at least had good ratings, including 8 out of 10 from Rotten Tomatoes, so it's probably worth a watch.

Melissa George and Michael Dorman thrill in this interesting, exciting, and chilling movie. The Triangle is a mind-bending outing. A small group of passengers is forced to vacate their damaged yacht and board a strange ocean liner. They soon realize their mistake. The ocean liner is not normal, and they get trapped in a tricky time loop. Their only option is to break free. Enjoy an exhilarating roller-coaster adventure full of mystery and thrills. Christopher Smith directed this very enjoyable thriller. It's a fun watch.

The Cruise

Finally, if you really want the full Bermuda Triangle Experience, you can take a cruise. One company, a Norwegian cruise company that offers "The Ancient Mysteries Cruise" guarantees a rather tongue-in-cheek full refund for patrons who vanish in the Bermuda Triangle. The next cruise, which begins from New York in March 2023, will travel the Atlantic Ocean and offers a fascinating tour of the dodgiest areas in the Bermuda Triangle in a glass-bottomed boat and access to lots of scientific lectures and question and answer sessions. It will hopefully meet its exciting mandate at approximately £ 1450.00 for the short cruise.

Fancy a Cruise? If you really want the full Bermuda Triangle Experience, you can take a cruise. One company, a Norwegian cruise company that offers "The Ancient Mysteries Cruise " guarantees a rather tongue-in-cheek full refund for patrons who vanish in the Bermuda Triangle. The next cruise, which begins from New York in March 2023, will travel the Atlantic Ocean and offers a fascinating tour of the dodgiest areas in the Bermuda Triangle in a glass-bottomed boat and access to lots of scientific lectures and question and answer sessions. It will hopefully meet its exciting mandate at approximately £ 1450.00 for the short cruise.

Fun Fact:

There is a whole range of Bermuda Triangle comics for comic fans. An entertaining one written by Chelsea Cain tells the story of a mysterious island teeming with supernatural conspiracies, demons, and horrible villains. The spy, Nora Freud, gets involved. She understands eighty-seven ways to murder someone with a toothpick, and she's already utilized thirty-two of them. The fun continues.

Fun Fact:

The Documentary Series "Into Cursed Waters" 2023 is a one-season 6-episode series looking at all the science and mystery behind the Bermuda Triangle. Each week an intrepid team endeavors to identify one mysteriously lost wreck and evaluate the evidence behind the mythologies and the science.

Questions:

1. What quirky offer does the Norwegian cruise company make?

2. The book by Gian Quasar is in the genre of which author?

3. In the movie Triangle, what traps the victims?

4. What does Nora Freud use to kill people?

5. How did Rotten Tomatoes rate Triangle?

Answers:

1. What quirky offer does the Norwegian cruise company make? **A money-back guarantee if the client vanished in the Bermuda Triangle.**

2. The book by Gian Quasar is in the genre of which author? **Charles Berlitz.**

3. In the movie Triangle, what traps the victims? **A time loop.**

4. What does Nora Freud use to kill people? **A toothpick.**

5. How did Rotten Tomatoes rate Triangle? **8 out of 10.**

CONCLUSION

"The ocean has always been a mysterious place to humans, and when foul weather or poor navigation is involved, it can be a very deadly place... There is no evidence that mysterious disappearances occur with any greater frequency in the Bermuda Triangle than in any other large, well-traveled area of the ocean."

-US Coast Guard.

We've heard it all in this article. We've heard the science, the myths, and the speculation. We've heard the theories, possible, probable, and absurd. Everybody reaches their own conclusions based on the evidence they find convincing or their personal belief system. The one thing that becomes very clear is whether or not the Bermuda Triangle is a place of supernatural mystery, death, and disappearances or whether it's just a very volatile and stormy area, or even if the information is skewed because of high traffic, it's going to remain a story of endless fascination to people.

We seldom encounter mysteries outside of movies and novels. Most of us are not explorers finding our own mysteries. Life is generally pretty dull and routine, pursuing the challenges of daily living. Compared to a tedious daily routine, the suggestion of a mystery, something hidden to discover, and create a greater knowledge about life, is enormously charming. It's a surprising and rare gift. And one which humankind loves to receive.

Mysteries, fictitious or actual, fully understood or barely implied, offer such richness. They enable us to be consumed by something other than our tedious lives, fulfill our curiosity, and allow us to appreciate the sense of realization and achievement that arises from turning random information into meaning. Mysteries also hold a sense of excitement because the world might just be a more wonderful and bizarre place than the mundane, well-known world we traverse daily.

If this is the case, then the most practical and convincing arguments that the Bermuda Triangle is a mere myth will not convince the average person because it will steal their dreams of a fascinating and amazing world out there, even if it is chilling at times.

BIBLIOGRAPHY

1. Lougheed R. The Bermuda Triangle Fact or Fiction. 5 May 2021 Ops Group.

   https://ops.group/blog/the-bermuda-triangle-fact-or-fiction/

2. Spark Notes. The Tempest. Updated 2022.

   https://www.google.com/search?q=ariels+words+the+tempest+1+2&oq=&aqs=chrome.14.69i58j69i176j69i64j35i39i362i523l12.-1j0j4&client=ms-android-vf-za-revc&sourceid=chrome-mobile&ie=UTF-8#sbfbu=1&pi=ariels%20words%20the%20tempest%201%202

3. National Museum of the US Navy. Updated 2022

   https://www.history.navy.mil/content/history/museums/nmusn/explore/photography/wwi/wwi-convoys/uss-cyclops-mystery-1918.html

4. De Abreu K Exploration Mysteries: The Disappearance of Joshua Slocum March 7, 2022,

   https://explorersweb.com/exploration-mysteries-disappearance-joshua-slocum/

5. Radford B. Bermuda Triangle: Where Facts Disappear September 25, 2012, Live Science

   https://www.livescience.com/23435-bermuda-triangle.html

6. Stimpson A 7 Chilling Conspiracy Theories about the Bermuda Triangle. April 18, 2022, Popular Mechanics

   https://www.popularmechanics.com/science/environment/

a39750723/what-is-the-bermuda-triangle/

7. Siddique A The Bermuda Triangle February 11, 2019, University of Ohio.

https://u.osu.edu/vanzandt/2019/02/11/the-bermuda-triangle/

Image License-Free

1. The Bermuda Triangle: The Bermuda Triangle is a place of strange happenings. Dozens of airplanes and ships have disappeared there for completely unexplained reasons. There have been ships disappearing without trace or distress signal, even in fair weather. A squadron of US navy bombers disappeared without a trace.

    https://commons.wikimedia.org/wiki/File:Bermuda_Triangle_map_%\28de%29.svg

2. Planes, Ships, and People Have All Disappeared without a Trace: Skeptics say that the Bermuda Triangle is all about myth and hype and that aircraft and vessels have regularly and mysteriously disappeared from other well-traveled sections of the ocean. They insist that people traverse that area safely on a daily basis. There are many people, however, who believe that the Bermuda Triangle is the Devil's Triangle. Even the explorer Christopher Columbus noted a flaming object

falling into the sea there and there have been scores of unexplained. events.

3. Joshua Slocum: After gaining extensive prestige as the first individual to sail solo around the world, Joshua Slocum vanished, with his boat The Spray, without a trace on a voyage from Martha's Vineyard to South America in 1909. Though it's uncertain what occurred, many sources later credited his loss to the mysterious Bermuda Triangle. Speculation was rife as to the cause as he was a family man and a fine sailor. Possibly one of the violent and sudden storms in the Bermuda Triangle caused his demise. Or possibly it was something more mysterious.

4. More Lost Souls- The famous Amelia Earhart, the first woman to successfully do a cross-Atlantic solo flight, was lost over the ocean too. Her final flight in January 1939 was thought to have come down in the Bermuda Triangle. She was never found.

Electra,_small.jpg

5. The Tempest- William Shakespeare's drama "The Tempest," some scholars of literature and history assert was based on a genuine Bermuda shipwreck. This may have strengthened the region's mysterious aura. However, rumors and reports of mysterious disappearances only captured the public's attention after the 20th century. This is possible because of improved communication.

    https://en.wikipedia.org/wiki/File:First-page-first-folio-tempest.jpg

6. The South Atlantic Anomaly: Also known as the SAA, (the outer space Bermuda Triangle) is an unexpectedly weak place in the Earth's magnetic field. Unfortunately, it seems to be growing and dividing into two sections. For people on Earth, the SAA generates no apparent harm at ground level but in space, this anomaly behaves like a "pothole" for spacecraft and satellites.

    https://en.wikipedia.org/wiki/South_Atlantic_Anomaly#/media/File:SAA_2020.png

7. Fancy a Cruise? If you really want the full Bermuda Triangle Experience, you can take a cruise. One company, a Norwegian cruise company that offers "The Ancient Mysteries Cruise " guarantees a rather

tongue-in-cheek full refund for patrons who vanish in the Bermuda Triangle. The next cruise, which begins from New York in March 2023, will travel the Atlantic Ocean and offers a fascinating tour of the dodgiest areas in the Bermuda Triangle in a glass-bottomed boat and access to lots of scientific lectures and question and answer sessions. It will hopefully meet its exciting mandate at approximately £ 1450.00 for the short cruise.

https://www.rawpixel.com/image/583243/nautical-leisure

About Us

At our core, we believe that history is more than just a subject to be learned. It's an experience to be had.

Our mission is to educate and inspire the next generation by providing them with a window into the fascinating and often surprising world of the past. We want to help young people make sense of the complexities of history and understand the lessons it has to offer.

By creating unforgettable encounters with relics of the past, we hope to ignite a lifelong passion for learning and discovery.

Thank you,